Christopher's Story:
An Indictment of the American Mental Health System

By John C. Rubisch, Ph.D.

Christopher's Story:
An Indictment of the American Mental Health System
Copyright ©2015 John C. Rubisch

ISBN 978-1622-879-76-2 PRINT
ISBN 978-1622-879-77-9 EBOOK

LCCN 2015946857

July 2015

Published and Distributed by
First Edition Design Publishing, Inc.
P.O. Box 20217, Sarasota, FL 34276-3217
www.firsteditiondesignpublishing.com

Some names and identifying details have been changed to protect the privacy
of individuals

This book is not intended as a substitute for the medical advice of physicians.
The reader should regularly consult a physician in matters relating to his/her
health and particularly with respect to any symptoms that may require
diagnosis or medical attention.

A father... a son ... a painful journey with a tragic ending. Christopher's Story will linger in your heart and mind long after you have finished reading it!

Debra McDonald,
Librarian

This family's harrowing experiences grab your heart and expose the tremendous deficiencies that still exist in the American mental health system.

Janet Ray,
AP English Teacher

Part biography, part social commentary, part cold case, a compelling tale of the author's descent into his son's problems and the madness of the country's mental health system.

Neil Mason,
Neil Mason Executive Search

A compelling and emotional story which provides stimulating insights into America's mental health system and one family's efforts to get it right. Great interest in following the struggles and outcomes.

Robert Beller M.S.
Licensed Psychologist

If you think you've read it all about mental health, sacrifice, human development or dads and sons, you haven't. 'Christopher's Story' is engagingly detailed, sad, honest, funny, emotional and balanced. You won't be disappointed - once you pick it up, it won't hit your night stand until you've finished.

Robert Biscontini
School Counselor/Psychologist

John C. Rubisch, Ph.D.

In my 35 years as a public school special needs teacher, I have witnessed much of the despair of which Dr. Rubisch writes. Should be required reading for anyone who has any contact with a special needs child.

Bruce Searfoss,
Retired Special Needs Teacher, Athletic Coach

This work is dedicated to the memory of Mateusz Bell. He did not have to die

Christopher's Story:
An Indictment of the American Mental Health System

Table of Contents

Preface

This is the story of my son, Christopher J. Rubisch. I do not condone his behaviors. I am not writing this to elicit sympathy.

Instead, I tell his story to call public attention to our failed mental health system in the United States. It is a story that is largely unknown. You can be angry with my son. You can also be angry about the American mental health system.

The information in this book comes from multiple resources:

➢ Tests: psychiatric, psychological, school, achievement. Chris was tested many, many, times over the years

➢ Records: from schools, mental health facilities, medical facilities, institutions, group homes, the legal system

➢ Anecdotal Reports: At various times in raising Chris, I kept a journal of what occurred. Keeping a journal was helpful to myself as I could reference when events occurred. More importantly, it was a necessity in dealing with the mental health system. When I would ask mental health (MH) for help on an emergency basis, they would give me a tablet and ask me to write down everything that happened in the last month. If it did not occur in the last month, it didn't count. If I was vague about a date, it would not count. Once I learned this, I was happy to hand them my notes and say, "How many pages do you need?"

John C. Rubisch, Ph.D.

The names of Chris, Diane Bell, Mateusz Bell as well as the names of the police officers, the chief medical examiner, and the assistant attorney general from New Hampshire are a matter of public record. Other names of individuals who are mentioned in this book have been changed. Although the behavior of some, particularly the MH professionals, may be extremely questionable, the focus of this book is on the system at large.

The Call

On August 28, 2006 at 9 PM, I received "the call." I always knew one day I would get "the call." But I also thought it would be from someone else telling me my son Christopher was dead or near dead.

Instead, it was from twenty-three year old Chris. Crying and difficult to understand, he was in Strafford County Prison in New Hampshire. He had been babysitting an infant. The baby started to cry and got on Chris's nerves. He spanked the baby and then he shook the baby. He said the baby was badly hurt. When the mother of the baby got back, he told her that the baby fell down the steps. The baby was taken to the hospital. Chris was saying that he did not deserve to live, he did not want a lawyer, and he did not want to talk to anyone. He was also on suicide watch. He gave me the name of a public defender to call. I suggested that he talk to a minister. I told him that I loved him, and he said that he loved me.

Although I had suspected something like this would occur for a long time, I was still devastated. I later learned the child my son abused was only eight months old. I was stunned as Chris's biological father abused him when he was just seven months old. Twenty-three years later the repetition of violence had come full circle despite my attempts to help my son through medication, counseling, and therapeutic residential placements. This is Christopher's story: an indictment of the American mental health system.

Beginnings

Christopher was born in Harrisburg, Pennsylvania on October 23, 1982. His biological parents were a young, unwed couple. The mother was about age sixteen, reportedly of below average intelligence. She was pretty, skinny, with long brown hair which hung in her face.

Christopher's father was a few years older. He was of average intelligence. At one point in his adolescence, he had been placed in an institutional setting due to family discord. He had an aversion to attending school.

Christopher was placed in foster care at age seven months. He was placed due to a broken clavicle. His father inflicted the injury. He had cigarette burns on his body also caused by his father. There was a burn scar on his chest reportedly caused by the spilling of hot tea. I once asked a caseworker about this. She said it was thought this might have been a case of abuse, but it could not be proved.

Chris stayed in the foster home until December of 1983 when he went to live with his maternal grandmother. He returned to his mother shortly thereafter. However, things had changed little, and he ended up back in foster care. He stayed with a working-class family for approximately eighteen months.

The rights of the birth parents were terminated, and Chris went to live in a home with a family that was to adopt him. They had a son that was two years older than Chris. However, they decided not to adopt him. My understanding was the mother had told the caseworker that she just "could not love" Chris.

He went back into foster care but not in the same home in which he had previously lived. In March of 1986 he was placed by an agency with my wife and me. He was three and a half at that time and had lived in six different family situations.

My wife and I had been married five years. She was older than I and was a widow with adult children from her previous marriage.

There were already signs in the early years of his life, before coming to live with us, that Chris had problems. When he was born his head circumference of 31.5 cm was small for the length of his body, 48.26 cm (19 in). At twenty-three months of age, an evaluation conducted by Polyclinic Hospital of Harrisburg indicated that he was behind in all areas of development with a high score of seventy-eight on fine motor behavior and a low score of fifty-two on personal social behavior. One hundred is considered average.

There was a follow-up audiological evaluation a month later. His receptive language skills were six months behind his chronological age. In the report it mentioned Chris was very moody and sensitive to discipline. He would frequently bang his head against the wall when he did not get his way.

Due to the head banging, Chris was referred to Albert Einstein Medical Center in Philadelphia for an evaluation in October of 1984. This was seventeen months before he came to live with us. He was banging his head two to three times a day. He was also eating excessively to the point that he was vomiting. At the evaluation it was determined that he was small for his size. His height was at the 30th percentile, his weight at the 25th percentile, his head circumference was less than the 5th percentile (50th percentile is average). During the evaluation he demonstrated head titubation (the swaying of the head on an intermittent basis). This can be a sign of brain disease. Einstein's final impression was that Chris's problems were due to "familial delay with secondary emotional and social deprivation." There is no indication that an X-ray or MRI was done.

At the age of twenty-nine months, Chris was again seen at the Polyclinic Hospital. As judged by the Gesell Developmental Schedule, he was significantly behind in Adaptive Behavior, Gross Motor Behavior, Personal Social Behavior, and Language Skills. The latter was his lowest score. Fine motor behavior was slightly above average. An evaluation a year later found his scores in these areas to be essentially the same.

My wife and I found Chris to be loveable and not the least bit wary of his new environment. Perhaps he had moved so many times he was immune to another change. However, we also discovered he was strong-willed and resistant to discipline. For example, if I placed him in time-out he would simply walk away. He would have severe temper tantrums, and we found it best to avoid direct confrontation by distracting him or manipulating the situation. He was oppositional. In one situation in which he was screaming at me, I told him to continue to scream. He immediately stopped. We also noticed he would not cry. On one occasion he fell face first onto a driveway. He got up without uttering a sound. Perhaps this was because he could never count on having someone to comfort him.

There were also problems at the day care center where he went during the day while we worked. At the age of three, he was biting other children and intentionally urinating on the floor. On one occasion he was caught choking another child.

Pennsylvania has educational organizations called Intermediate Units to assist special needs children. The Intermediate Unit saw Chris in September of 1986 for another evaluation. Again it was found he was delayed compared to norms for his age. Sequencing was difficult for him. Consequently, he was unable to use his imagination in play to develop a theme. Also, he was unable to speak in sequences longer than two words, unable to repeat sentence sequence repetitions that were spoken to him, and unable to listen to a sequenced story and answer questions.

Chris was adopted in October 24, 1986. Mostly because of the stress Chris brought into our lives, things were not good between my wife and me. My father had taught me one could just put his mind to something and get anything done. Although I tried to be Superman, I was not. Shortly after the adoption, we separated and eventually got divorced. I received custody of Chris. I remember Chris crying and saying that he was going to lose another mommy. I told him that would not happen. We would still see Mommy, but before too long, my wife dropped out of the picture.

I thought I would get married again before too long. I wanted to be married. My belief was that women would look at me and see a compassionate man caring for his son. What they did see was I was part of a package deal, and the smaller package had big problems, which were only just emerging. I would never marry again.

At this point I thought Chris was the way he was because others had rejected him. It was my mother who would be the first to hypothesize that others rejected him because he was the way he was.

On Our Own

Being a single parent was something I never anticipated. I had figured I would be the secondary parent with a wife being the primary care provider. I was raised to be all those male words that start with "a": aggressive, achieve, assert, advance, attack. I found what my four-year old son needed was for me to be there for him. I remember telling a friend I wish we could fast forward to the age of eight so we could play catch in the back yard.

My life was not turning out the way I envisioned it. I was living with a child with many problems in the middle of nowhere. Television and even radio reception was sporadic, and a weekly trip to the grocery store required some forethought. I remember waking up one Saturday morning and just sobbing in utter frustration.

I was a guidance counselor at Susquenita High School in Perry County north of Harrisburg, Pennsylvania. We went to live in an apartment over a farmhouse a few miles from the school. During the day while I was at school, Chris went to a day care center. He was labeled as bad. He hit and bit. He did not conform to group activities and sometimes refused to participate. At times he walked out of time out.

In February of 1987 at the age of four years and five months, the Intermediate Unit reevaluated him. In many areas he had improved markedly over the previous evaluation six months ago. He was able to name alphabet letters. Previously, he had been unable to do so. There was improvement in gross motor items, a finger-thumb opposition task (touching the tips of the fingers with the thumbs), and visual matching.

In other areas however, there was still need for improvement. Although he could rote count to at least twelve, he was unable to demonstrate meaningful counting greater than one. He refused letter and shape copying activities and a request to write his name. He had difficulty with block building tasks using more than three blocks.

At their recommendation we began play therapy at Polyclinic Hospital. The concept of play therapy is that young children, lacking the verbal skills to benefit from counseling, can express themselves through play. In this way play will be a therapeutic process.

The hospital had a playroom set up for this process. The child was able to select from a number of play alternatives such as toys, crayons, and dolls. We were to replicate this process at home. I would set up the kitchen with the play options we saw at the playroom. Chris would always select the same thing to do: pour water from one container to another. He would do this continuously without moving to another toy. As instructed I was to be with him but let him take the lead so as not to interfere with his natural inclinations. Perhaps I would talk to him about what he was doing, but I was never direct his play or move his attention to something else. In the end I found the play therapy to be totally ineffective.

Play was a problem for Chris. He could not do it. As stated before he was unable to do representational play. If I would play with him and construct a tale of his stuffed animals interacting with each other, he would enjoy it. However, if left to himself, he could not do the same. Instead, he would throw the toys around the room. As a single parent this had a great influence on the way we lived at home. As Chris was unable to entertain himself, I had to monitor him at home continuously. If I went to clean one room, he would be destroying another room. A favorite activity for Chris was to stand on his head on the sofa. Often this resulted in a lamp being knocked off an adjoining end table when he lost his balance.

Consequently, we spent a great deal of time away from home. In the summer we lived at the swimming pool. In the winter we would go to movies and the Museum of Scientific Discovery. MSD was a hands-on museum for children, but for the most part, it served as an indoor playground for Chris. Playgrounds were very forgiving. In the winter despite the freezing temperatures, we would often be at a park.

I remember one day at the park that did not go well. Chris was playing with a boy and got into what appeared to me a fairly typical childhood squabble. The other boy's mother appeared from seemingly nowhere and scooped him up. She said, in reference to Chris, that he was a boy whose parents obviously did not know how to raise him.

That remark set off all my parental inadequacy alarms, of which I had many, given all the problems inherent in raising Chris. My first thought was to fire an insult back at the woman, but seeing that Chris was crying, I knew the better thing was to console him.

In the few short months since my wife and I split, my life had changed immensely. Simple things became difficult or impossible. Once I wanted to buy a new stereo. I was unable to concentrate on what the salesperson was saying because Chris was pulling the knobs off television sets. Fairly simple errands would require me to leave him at the day care center or perhaps even get a baby sitter.

Chris's rambunctiousness was a problem other places as well. When we attended church he would roll around the floor and crawl underneath the pews. I would try to use the church nursery as an alternative. However, inevitably someone would march him upstairs to the sanctuary to me and, with a look of relief on her face, say Chris was too old to be in the nursery.

Before I encountered Chris's natural turbulence, I had sworn that I would never park my child in front of the television to entertain him. But when Chris reached a certain age, I discovered the saving power of the Teenage Mutant Ninja Turtles. However, Chris was so active that even televised cartoons were not always sufficient to maintain his attention.

Once a friend came to visit me. I told the friend that he was going to have to let Chris maintain control of the television. I went upstairs. About five minutes later I heard a crashing sound. I knew what had happened. Despite my warning my friend had turned the television to a sporting event. In response Chris had become active and knocked something over. My friend asked how I watched sports on TV. I gave him a simple response: I didn't. If I really wanted to watch something, I would tape it, try to avoid hearing the result, and watch it after Chris went to sleep at night. This scenario was rather ironic in that my relationship with my own father was built on watching sports on television. I looked forward to doing the same with my son, but Chris's inability to sit still prevented that from ever happening.

Bedtime was a continuous struggle. I would put him to bed and return to the living room. Chris would pop back out of his bedroom. On one occasion after a particularly long day, I was just falling asleep when I heard him in the bathroom. I went into the room to discover that he had smashed both my contact lenses for no apparent reason. I have an unusual problem with my eyes. I have to wear special contacts that are both expensive and hard to obtain. Without them, I should not drive.

When I discovered what happened to my lenses, I was so angry. I could feel myself getting physical pains in my stomach.

Christopher's Story:
An Indictment Of The American Mental Health System

If I had not had a girlfriend to call, I do not know if we would have survived that night.

Getting Chris going in the morning was always a problem as well. One morning I decided to use a stuffed-animal, a parrot, to talk to him while he was half asleep. It was during the Winter Olympics, and Parrot wanted to join Chris on his bobsled. The bobsled was Chris's bed. Parrot would try to worm himself underneath Chris's body but would always insist that he needed a "little more room." His requests were first polite, but he would slowly become more agitated. Eventually, by using my arms, Parrott would roll Chris out of bed with the three of us tumbling down the imagined bobsled track. Chris enjoyed this immensely and would insist on Parrot waking him up every day. Parrot would become an instrument of therapy. For example, if Chris had a bad day at school, the next morning Parrot would tell Chris of his bad day in school, which was always a little worse than Chris's day. Chris would laugh at this.

Despite the struggles and challenges, there were other times when Chris could be loveable. I remember reading to him while he sat on my lap. Sometimes when he was upset and in need of comfort, he would ask me to read to him. On one occasion when we were reading, he was preoccupied with a minor bruise he had on his toe and said, "Ow, my toe hurts." From then on when we were reading I would occasionally inject that phrase in stories. "Then the bear said 'Ow, my toe hurts.'" In response, Chris would laugh and give me a playful jab with his elbow. At moments like this I would feel wonderful, thinking that fatherhood was turning out the way I had always thought it would be.

Elementary Years

Kindergarten year, 1988-89, was relatively uneventful. Report cards stated that Chris needed improvement in the following areas: writing, coloring, cutting, remaining in seat at appropriate times, working and playing cooperatively, and keeping hands, feet, and objects to self. In her final remarks for the year, the teacher wrote, "We are hoping to see more improvement in Christopher's attitude and behavior in our classroom!" This statement was truly portentous.

Almost immediately Chris had problems in first grade. The school counselor observed him in class:

> Chris walked over to a girl seated in the middle of the classroom. He wanted her book. She put the book in her lap, under her desk. Chris made faces in her face and walked away. He made mocking noises to a boy passing him. The boy tried to reach back and kick Chris. Chris wanted the teacher to see his finished bird. He ran over and showed it to her. She complimented him on his bird, but asked about the coloring of the worm. He said that he only had to color half the worm green. Another student said something about doing the trash. (Chris had asked to do this earlier.) Chris ran over and grabbed the can. He was asked to put it back and was told that students

would do their own trash. He ignored the directions and began carrying the can around, doing trash. Chris began throwing the garbage in the can at other students. The teacher again asked him to put the trash can back. He ignored her. She walked up and helped carry the can over to where it belonged and (Chris) yelled on the way, "I'm going to keep it until I die." The teacher announced recess. He said, 'Oh goody' and ran to the teacher's desk. Chris took a Rubik's cube and returned to his seat (apparently he was not supposed to do this).

His teacher said of Chris, "His temper is out of this world when he goes off." Although I should not have been, I was shocked by this remark. After all I had seen his tantrums at home. But in my mind school was different. My son could not be behaving this way in school. However, he was.

His behavior was also dangerous. Angry with a boy on the playground, Chris reached under the boy's glasses and pressed on his eye. Once as a passenger in a moving vehicle, he had a temper tantrum. He accidently kicked the gearshift with his flailing feet and put the car in another gear.

The school counselor thought that Chris might have ADHD. In the fall of 1989, a psychiatrist evaluated him. (Note: at this time we also moved from the farmhouse to the small town of Marysville, which was in the school district where I worked.) I told the psychiatrist that Chris had no respect for authority and would not back down in a confrontation. Chris told the psychiatrist that he liked getting in fights, and there were problems because he would not stay in bed when it was bedtime. He said he did not listen to his teacher because he did not want to do so.

Christopher's Story:
An Indictment Of The American Mental Health System

The psychiatrist asked him if he could be granted a wish what would it be. Chris said not to be bad. When asked what made him mad, he said when he could not get his way and when his dad would not listen to him. The psychiatrist administered a test during which Chris was asked to draw a house, a tree, and a person. His findings:

> Chris's house tree person drawing was reminiscent of that which might be expected of a younger child. However, in addition, there were distortions particularly of the human figure, with huge balloon like appendages for hands, and six semi-circles which were supposed to be the fingers. The body was represented by two straight lines extending from a circle which was the head, the body also therefore representing the legs. He drew darkened circles for feet. There were no facial characteristics. He did not draw any windows nor other details in the house except for a door without a knob.

These distortions were a sign of organicity, or brain damage. However, I did not know it at the time, and it was not explained to me. Instead, I asked the psychiatrist about mixed dominance. Chris did most things with his right hand but kicked a ball with his left foot. In writing Chris would start with his left hand, and as he progressed across the paper, would switch to his right hand to finish the line. The doctor was non-committal about mixed dominance being an issue.

The diagnosis was ADHD, especially in group situations, with some oppositional tendencies. Play therapy and a prescription for Imipramine 10 mg were also recommended.

In retrospect this first contact with a child psychiatrist was an example of all those we were to see in the mental health system in the years Chris was growing up. Play therapy? Been there, done that. It didn't work. I came to learn that psychiatrists put children on the lowest level of a psychotropic drug possible. The low dosage was said to guard against the possibility of negative side effects. A cynic might add it would guard against the possibility of lawsuits if there were any extreme negative side effects. Time and again Chris would be given a low level of medication that would prove to be totally ineffective.

As for the diagnosis of ADHD, the late eighties was the time of the great ADHD wave, or as it was called back then, ADD. Seemingly every student that had a behavioral problem in my school was ADD and was prescribed medicine (most of the time Ritalin). Chris got on the tsunami and became ADD as well.

In early 1990 Chris was on medication for ADD. He was now eight years old. An observational report from the school counselor indicates that his behavior at school had not changed in the least:

March 13, 1990
Observation in classroom 17 from 10:31 to 11:04

10:34

Chris was sitting in his chair, making farting noises with his mouth and leaning back. His back was against the student's desk located behind him and his toes were barely keeping him balanced under his desk. Chris was calling out an incorrect word to the student located behind him. He was rocking in his chair.

10:36

Chris was putting his feet on the girl (a different girl from last observation) sitting next to him, she was yelling at Chris to stop it.

The teacher called on Chris to read the next sentence. He read and answered the question loudly. The answer was chickie.

10:37

Chris got out of his seat and walked back and forth in a six feet area like a chickie. He also made the noises. The other students laughed. He was asked to sit down, he did. Chris scribbled all over the bottom of the opposite blank page with a pencil.

10:44

He sat in his seat. Chris put his foot in his desk, raised his pant leg, bit on his knee, and tied his shoe. He got out of his seat to get a pair of scissors and a container of glue. He returned to his seat and spun the glass bottle around on his desk. He was asked not to do that. The teacher stopped it with her hand.

10:45

Chris was playing with the scissors. He was spinning them in his hand like a gun while standing. He walked up to a girl and touched her on her side. She hit him. He talked to a boy two seats behind him. Chris was asked to go to his seat, he did.

10:46

He had the scissors open and told the girl next to him that he was going to poke her with this (the scissors). Chris had the scissors in a stabbing position. He put the scissor point up against her arm.

10:47

Chris was wildly cutting up the side of his assignment paper. He was told to read the directions. He had to do steps one through six, before he needed the scissors. He said, "I don't care."

10:48

Chris had his pencil out of his desk, pointed it at the girl and said, "on guard." He made a comment about butt to the girl. In response to a conversation with the girl he said, "blue, you dumb, dumb."

10:55

He was doing karate moves with his hands and feet while balancing on his chair. Chris got out of his seat and stood behind the girl. She ignored him. He walked over to another student, who was coloring, and said, "Willy scribble, scrabble." The student got upset. Chris went to the front of the room for something and on his way back he called the same boy a "faggot." Chris returned to his seat. He sang "Willy, Scribble, Scrabble" loudly three times. The other student was yelling.

Chris was asked to stop and did. A different student on the other side of the room said something and Chris yelled, "I want you to shut up."

10:58

Chris got out of his seat and went over to the teacher. She stopped the individual work she was doing with a student to answer his question. He wanted to know if when he was finished with his assignment, he could play a game. (Chris had just heard the teacher tell another student that he could read a book quietly after he finished.) She said no, games are for recess; you'll need to read a book when you're finished. He went back to his seat grumbling that he didn't want to read a book. Chris talked to the girl next to him and said, "I don't care, my underwear. I bet twenty bucks I say that to my dad."

11:00

The student teacher gave Chris a direction. He talked back. He said "We don't have to because we're taking it home." Chris was singing a song about the girl sitting next to him off and on. He spelled "d-i-c-k" and asked the girl if she knew what that spelled. She said yes. He wanted her to say it. She said she wouldn't because she didn't want to get in trouble. Chris sang, "Fraidy cat, fraidy cat."

As was the practice of the day, Chris took achievement tests in the spring of 1990. He scored average or just below average in all areas.

In the fall of 1990, Chris began second grade. Because of his behavioral problems, he was given a psychological exam. On the Wechsler Intelligence Scale for Children-Revised (WISC-R), he scored a 103 on the verbal scale and a 77 on the performance. The mean test score for both scales is 100. The verbal part of the test examines areas such as vocabulary, comprehension, and information. The performance section has subsections in block design, picture concepts, and picture completion.

Chris's scores were an unusual combination. He was doing much better in school academically than would be expected. The psychologist credited me for this overachievement. Given his continued behavioral problems at school and home, it hardly made me feel better. The report concluded, "Chris is not your typical socially or emotionally disturbed student, and his behaviors should be manageable in a regular classroom at this time." Also buried in his report was the following: "Bender- 2 to 3 years below age and is usually associated with individuals with organic or perceptual difficulties."

As I was to learn later, this was a missed red flag. On the Bender-Gestalt tests, children are asked to draw figures. Those that have difficulty doing so, often have organic difficulties, or in more common language, brain damage. Recall that Chris had trouble drawing the House Tree Person test the previous year.

Along with medication Chris started therapy in 1990. Counseling would be a constant for his entire life. It was and still is a major tenet that people be treated by both counseling and psychotropic medication. We saw Ian Ingram, a therapist, at Holy Spirit Hospital. Ingram had us begin a behavioral modification program. Chris would receive points for good behavior during the week. If he earned sufficient points, we would eat at McDonalds on Friday night. The program did not work very well. The criteria was supposed to be positive behavior, but in reality, it was the absence of negative behavior: temper tantrums, defiance, not staying in bed, etc. Also behavior was difficult to both quantify and qualify. Problem behavior occurred often. I once said to a therapist that we had had a bad day. The therapist asked how often we had a bad day. I said, "For us, or for other people? For other people, every other day. For us, one of every five days. You get used to some of this stuff." What would be considered bad for others became part of our norm.

There was also a qualitative aspect. Is a temper tantrum that last ten minutes worth a point if only because it is not a temper tantrum of one half hour? Chris would get beyond the point he could control himself. In these cases it was frequently best for me to disengage. Once when he was having a tantrum, I turned on the television and sat down. He asked what I was doing, and I said watching cartoons. Chris disengaged and watched cartoons. When throwing a tantrum Chris would often become destructive. Sometimes when he got this way, I would attempt to stop him by physically restraining him. At other times I would just let him go and clean things up afterwards. On one occasion, as had been suggested by a friend, I walked outside to the backyard and left Chris to himself until his rage ran out. This did not work. He locked me out of the house. I thought I was going to have to break a window to get in, but Chris eventually relented and unlocked the door.

Many times when Chris got angry, he would tear up photos of me or of the two of us together. I have very few photos of myself from this time period in my life. The tantrums did not disappear when he got older. We tried many medications over the year, but none enabled Chris to control either his anger or his defiance.

Second grade, 1990-91, was marginally better at school than the previous year, primarily due to the teacher. There were two types of teachers in Chris's educational career. The first would be those that would receive an explanation of his problems, would say that they understood, and subsequently, would give him additional consideration. The second would be those that would receive an explanation of his problems, they would say that they understood, and would continue with no changes. In the case of the latter, standards and procedures for both academics and behavior were exactly that, and if he could not adhere to them, then he was the problem.

The latter attitude was certainly the one possessed by the Latchkey program, which was a before and after school program for elementary children at the school. I had to move him out of the program to a baby sitter.

Friends and family also fell into the two categories of compassionate and not. My mother was my backup, and Chris and I certainly would not have survived without her. Although she lived two hours away, she was always available to babysit, make homemade cookies with Chris, and to just listen to my frustrations on the phone. When I would compare Chris to myself as a boy, she would say he's not you. It took me awhile to realize her wisdom.

On the other hand, I remember talking to an old college buddy on the phone. I mentioned an event that he could not recall. To help his memory I reminded him that I had written about the event in my Christmas card to him. He responded that he never read my Christmas cards because he found my accounts of life with Chris to be too depressing.

In second grade medication was problematic for Chris. It was supposed to be effective for three hours. However, sometimes it would take an hour to kick in. If there was a delay in it taking effect, he did not necessarily get three hours of its effectiveness. The only guarantee was he would be like a zombie. However, he was a zombie that was still capable of losing control if he had to face adversity.

Medication would also kill his appetite. A considerable amount of time and effort was spent in adjusting the type of medication and the timing of the medication to best fit with the school and meal schedule. For example, it was found that Chris would often have trouble early in the morning before school began. The bus would arrive at the elementary school, but the students would stay onboard because the teachers had yet to arrive. Could there be a more chaotic situation than a bus full of kids with nothing to do? So we changed his medication schedule to ensure it was in his system for the AM bus situation. However, we still had to work around meal times. Consequently we were eating supper at 3 P.M. when I returned from school. I remember crying in frustration because I did not want to eat my evening meal midway through the afternoon.

The school year of 1990-91, when Chris was eight and in second grade, saw the advent of a new negative behavior: stealing. He stole at the babysitter, at school, in stores, anywhere. If Chris wanted something, he stole it. At a store Chris was caught stealing pogs and candy. The store pressed charges, and we were referred to the justice system. Subsequently, we attended a Saturday session, which was supposed to be therapeutic in nature.

Chris told the people at the Saturday session he stole the items because I would not buy them for him. I would give Chris an allowance always with the same stipulation: he could squander the money immediately, or he would wait a week, and I would double it. Chris's response was always the same, "Squander." When he got much older, I would joke that he would buy a sack of his own excrement if someone would sell it to him just to get rid of the money. He agreed.

Notes from Chris's therapy sessions with Ian Ingram indicate that he was very hyperactive during the sessions. Ingram would attempt to review Chris's goals with him, but one must wonder how successful this could be with my son's hyper state. Hope was placed on adjusting the type, amount, and timing of the medications. There was no significant difference whether the dosage or the medication itself was changed. Throughout his childhood we continuously sought the magic elixir of psychotropic medications that would solve his problems. We never found it.

At the age of eight, fighting, impulsiveness, defiance, biting other children, and opposition to doing homework in the evenings, marked Chris's behavior. In therapy he could identify his behavioral goals, but he could not execute them in the outside world. Chris's achievement test results were in the average range for second grade.

In the late summer of 1991, Chris went out for football. I was skeptical, but he wanted to play as other boys he knew were doing so. It was a total disaster. The coaches complained to me constantly about his behavior. Part of the problem was Chris was not complying with their wishes, part was teasing and pranks by the other boys, and part was Chris did not or could not understand the concept of the game. Used as cannon fodder on the defensive line against bigger boys, Chris would run away from the blocker rather than get hit while trying to pursue the ball carrier. After about a month I realized that Chris was not going to change, and the coaches were not going to change their perception that he was the problem. As much as I hated to have him quit anything, it was what we had to do. Chris played what he understood was his last game, at which he served as captain, and his season was over. The team went on to play six more weeks, but I don't think Chris ever knew.

Chris took swimming lessons and karate during his elementary years. Lacking the collaborative aspect of team sports, they both went much better for him.

Chris's third grade year, 1991-92, was no better than the previous year: more fighting, defiance, stealing, impulsiveness, hyperactivity, and explosive temper outbursts. In one therapy appointment with Ian Ingram, Chris was running down the hallway, climbing under chairs, and crawling on the floor. Yet in April of 1992, the psychiatrist who was in charge of his medication noted that Chris was doing "quite well" although he noted there were a few fights with other children. His response was to increase Chris's medication by 5 mg. We were drowning in problems. Instead of a life preserver, he threw us a candy lifesaver.

Christopher's Story:
An Indictment Of The American Mental Health System

In July of 1992 Chris attended church camp. I was asked to pick him up early as he was out of control. There were verbal confrontations. He was also hyperactive and controlling toward his peers. On the way home Chris cried and asked me why the other kids did not like him.

In August of 1992, another psychologist, Ivan York, saw Chris. On the Wide Range Achievement Test (WRAT-R) Chris's Verbal IQ was 86, his Performance 90, his Full Scale 87. The mean, in each case, is 100. The conclusion of the psychologist was that Chris was ADHD, with both verbal and math learning disabilities, and he had poor impulse control. Additionally, the Bender Gestalt test, which had previously been administered two years earlier, gave strong evidence of brain injury. This time, perhaps because the words brain damaged were used or perhaps because the report came from a psychologist I respected, the result of the Bender made a bigger impression on me. On me but not others. It would be another four years before a medical professional would focus on the possibility that brain damage was the root of Chris's problems.

The 1992-93 school year saw some changes, not in Chris, but in his situation. I stopped utilizing Ian Ingram and the concomitant psychiatric services at Holy Spirit Hospital. Chris had not improved. I felt that too much of the therapy session was focused on me: was I finding time for myself, did I have a structured routine, etc. Routine was not a problem as Chris loved routine. Once, when we went to the store to buy groceries, we pulled out of the driveway and turned in the opposite direction of the store. Chris panicked and blurted out, "I thought we're going to get groceries!" I explained that we were going to run an errand before groceries. He calmed down.

One does not get more structured than me. However, if bedtime was 9:00 and I did not have him in bed until 9:02, I was told that I had to keep to the time schedule. In stressing myself out over the two minutes, I would make matters worse.

Due to our termination of services with Holy Spirit, there was a written discharge summary report from the psychiatrist. Dated

November 11, 1992, it was just amazing in its conclusion. In talking about the medication Chris received it was stated "The effect was quite noticeable and he seemed to be quite responsive to it in terms of concentration and attention span, physical hyperactivity as well as impulse control." This was written despite pages and pages from Ian Ingram noting the opposite.

Reality as well belied the rosy picture painted by the psychiatrist. Things were as bad as they had ever been at home and at school. At some point during the 1992-93 school year (I do not have the exact date), Chris started a fire in the house. I had bought an igniter for a barbecue grill. Knowing Chris's fascination with such things, I locked the igniter in a box. I woke the next day to the smell of smoke in the air and to find that the box had been jimmied open. I found the igniter, Chris, and the burning material all in close proximity to each other on the first floor of the house. After extinguishing the materials, I gathered my wits, briefcase, and Chris together and headed out the backdoor toward the car to go to school. I was only a little way up the road when it occurred to me that I had not investigated the entire house before leaving. When I asked Chris he said he had been in the basement. Imagining our house in flames, I made a u-turn and proceeded as fast as possible to home. Drivers stopped in a traffic jam blasted their horns as I passed them on the shoulder. I arrived at the house to find a smoldering rag in the basement.

Things were also bad at school. Chris's main teacher in fourth grade was one that lacked compassion for his problems. Homework was overwhelming. Here is an example: on a spelling pretest, Chris missed eighteen of twenty words. Consequently, his homework assignment was to write each one of the missed words twenty times. Many of the words were over ten letters long. One was Prometheus. We struggled through writing the 360 words. Near completion of the assignment

Chris said, "Oh, I forgot. We were supposed to write them in alphabetical order." We did not rewrite them in alphabetical order. I resisted the temptation to send a note to the teacher saying although I had a Master's degree and was working on a doctorate, I had never had occasion to write the word Prometheus.

Chris continued to have problems behaviorally in school. On one occasion I was called to the school because Chris had run out of class and then out of the building. When I asked him why, he told me that a girl was teasing him. He got very angry and was going to hit her. However, he realized he could not do that. Seeing no other alternative he ran out of the building to avoid hitting her.

As the result of the deterioration of the school situation, the decision was made to place Chris at a partial hospitalization program during the day. He would receive education and therapy in a nurturing setting with only a few other children present.

That sure sounds good. In reality, in my experience as a parent and a counselor, these placements are mostly to get the troubled child out of the school so the other students can learn. Hours are shorter than regular school, education less intensive, and therapy can vary widely in quality and quantity. In most cases therapy is done in a group. The rationale given for group is that the patients can learn from each other and develop social skills. This strategy is questionable given that the reason for their inclusion in the group in the first place is that they lack social skills. A cynic may think a group also means that an institution can collect multiple fees while only utilizing one or perhaps two therapists.

Chris did not get significantly better or worse when he was at the partial program. After a few months there, we had a discharge meeting. Many theories were discussed in regards to his problems. One of them was that he was suffering from Traumatic Stress Disorder. After an hour one individual stood up, announced time had run out on her parking meter, and she had to leave. Another person also got up and said she had another appointment. I lost it at that point. I said angrily that Chris had been there for months, they had been unable to reach any conclusions on how to help him, and now the meeting was over because of a parking meter. My statement had no effect; the meeting was over.

There is an epilogue on the partial placement, which would be funny if it was not so sad. At the discharge meeting the staff emphasized repeatedly the need for Chris to attend the program until his last scheduled day, which was a Friday. It was important psychologically for "closure." That Friday there was a big snowstorm. Consequently, there was no school or school provided transportation to the program. I called on the following Monday to find out about Chris going in for his last day. I was told that his last day was Friday even though he had not been able to attend. When I asked about his closure, they repeated that his last day was Friday. One might surmise that the last day insurance was covering Chris's placement was on Friday, and closure be damned.

After his discharge from the partial program, Chris returned to his regular school placement but with another teacher. Mrs. Perez had a fearsome reputation as a teacher, and initially, this might have seemed to be a poor choice. However, the day before he returned, Mrs. Perez told her class that Chris was coming back, and if there were any problems, she would hold them responsible for setting him up to go off. There were no major problems for the rest of the year.

Leaving the partial program also meant Chris needed a new provider for therapy and medication. In March of 1993 we started to see a new organization in the area, Transact. I had heard great things about their work with children. Their initial diagnosis of Chris:

1. Temperament- High activity, irregular rhythmicity, high distractibility, approach, slow to adapt, short persistence, medium intensity, low threshold
2. Readiness- Inefficient reading, math and written expression
3. Attention- Low arousal, impulsive, inefficient filtering, inefficient monitoring, inefficient problem solving, inefficient verbal mediation, inefficient scanning
4. Neuromaturation- Soft signs present indicate neuromaturational delay/difference suggests biological basis for attentional weaknesses. Meets criteria for Attention Deficit Disorder
5. Stresses- Multiple stresses
6. Comparisons- Low self-awareness, low self-esteem, absence of locus of control, poor motivation

They placed a major emphasis on the irregular rhythmicity. The idea was that most people have and want a regular rhythm in their life. Chris did not have that. Number 4, Neuromaturation is also worth noting because of "biological basis for attentional weakness." Once again, the possibility of a problem with his brain pops up. Once again, it was ignored. Transact did ADHD and Chris was put on the assembly line for ADHD treatment.

One thing I liked about Transact was that they insisted Chris receive Ritalin and not the cheaper generic alternative. There was a difference. The generic did not always work as well.

It did not "kick-in" on time or sometimes at all. Ritalin was more dependable.

There was another thing that was new with Transact. They said that many of these children had bowel problems. It was related to their irregular rhythmicity. In Chris's case this was true. He would have huge bowel movements. I learned to break them up with a plunger before flushing lest the toilet become backed up. There was one memorable Christmas Eve when I failed to do so, and I spent the evening clearing the backup.

Transact's solution to this problem was to regularly give Chris medication to clean out his system. My mother, a nurse, was skeptical as it was the same medication used for patients for surgery. It worked to the extent that it cleaned out his system. However, after taking the medication, Chris would be in great pain, with tears rolling down his cheeks while sitting on the toilet. One time it got to be too much for me, and I promised that we would never use it again. And we didn't. When Transact would ask if we were still using the bowel cleaner, I would lie and say yes. In reality I gave him a laxative. Neither the bowel cleaner nor the laxative made any difference. Many years later as an adult, Chris told me the cause of his chronic constipation was that he simply did not want to stop whatever activity in which he was engaged to go to the bathroom.

We saw Transact from March of 1993 to August of 1996 when Chris was ten to thirteen years of age. Every few months we would see the psychiatrist who would tweak Chris's meds. There was no appreciable difference in Chris's behavior. I remember seeing a strange look on the psychiatrist's face at times, and I wonder if he sensed there was something else going on with Chris. If so he never said anything.

We saw two different therapists for counseling. After a while I became totally disillusioned with talk therapy. They always wanted to talk with me: were we keeping a schedule they would ask, he must have structure they would repeat. At one point I talked about how hectic mornings were before we would get out the door. The therapist asked me to list the order of things we did in the morning. I refused. I could not see whether if I brushed my teeth before I shaved would make any difference. I told her that I was well adjusted to society, while Chris was not.

At the next therapy session, she said that the therapeutic team had discussed our situation, and they thought it would be best if I put Chris up for adoption. I imagine this was supposed to shock me, and it did. As stated before I had feelings that many parents have of being inadequate and being afraid that others would notice. For me it was even worse as I was a school counselor, and I was often advising other parents about their children. I always feared someone would say something to the effect of you can't even raise your own kid (I only remember this actually happening once). Eventually, when someone would come to me and inform me of yet another misdeed by Chris, I learned to say thank you for letting me know, I'll take care of it, good-bye.

As for Transact I decided at that point I was going to have to play along with the therapy game if only to get Chris's medication. I was still seeking that magic elixir to turn him into a normal boy.

As we began at Transact in the spring of 1993, Chris was achieving at or near grade level on achievement tests. His final report grades for fourth grade were mostly Ds and Ss (satisfactory).

In fifth and sixth grade, Chris was placed in a special education classroom for students with emotional problems in a neighboring school district. This type of classroom was shared by the area schools as there insufficient numbers of students in each individual district to offer that class within the district. In my experience spending as little money as possible has always been the driving force in regular and special education. An example of this was Chris's transportation arrangements to get to the neighboring school district. Chris informed me that the van picked him up in the morning and went south. I responded that he was wrong; it had to go north as that was the direction for his school. However, Chris was insistent it went south. One night we went to a basketball game in the direction that Chris claimed his van went. He was able to pick out landmarks along the way. I concluded that he had been right about the van. I asked someone in school transportation about this. Incredibly, the van took a circuitous route to school going south, west, north, and then east before ending up at the school. A trip that would have taken 25 minutes via the shortest direct route, took three times that long! The reason? Only one van was used to pick up all the children. Seventy-five minutes with a van full of special needs children. God bless the driver.

In fifth grade Chris found himself in a smaller classroom with children who were more like himself and with a more understanding teacher, Mrs. Williams. Behaviorally, Chris had fewer problems. This was not necessarily because Chris had improved, but because the teacher was more tolerant of his misdeeds. Perhaps not surprisingly with the special needs placement, his achievement scores dipped in the spring of 1994.

All of his scores were below grade level. Some of them were substantially below. An exception was his social studies score, which was at the twelfth grade level. This test consisted of reading charts, graphs, and maps. To me it meant Chris excelled when there was no sequencing involved as there would be with a language or math task.

In sixth grade, 1994-95, Chris remained at the special needs classroom in the neighboring school district. He was mainstreamed for some of his major classes. One of his teachers was Mr. Smith, a young man just out of college who towered over the children at six foot five. Chris idolized Mr. Smith. With the continued support from Mrs. Williams, he had his best year ever in education. Chris's grades were for the most part As and Bs, with Cs in Language and Art. He had a satisfactory in Phys Ed and earned another S in behavior.

One of the ironic things about special needs education is that once a child does well in a setting, the system wants to return the child to the previous school placement where the child was dysfunctional. Such was the case for Chris: now that he is improved, let's return him to regular education. My initial reaction was negative. Why return him to an environment where he has proven that he could not make it? A cynic might think it was because it was cheaper to educate him in a regular education classroom than one for special needs. I was asked the following question often during Chris's educational career: what is he capable of doing? By this time I had learned to answer it was irrelevant as Chris was not going to work to his capabilities because of his problems. However, still possessed with the idea that the professionals knew special education best, I agreed for Chris to return to regular ed in his home district for seventh grade, the 1995-96 school year.

The results were predictable. His grades plummeted. Behavioral problems increased. No one knew what to do with him. At times he was suspended from school. On these occasions I would have to leave him with a babysitter. Although he was thirteen I could not trust him alone.

After one suspension I asked the assistant principal what was the purpose of the suspension. If it was to teach Chris a lesson, that would not happen. He would be just as likely to misbehave the next time given the same circumstances. If it was to encourage his family to engage in corrective actions like counseling or medication, we were already doing so. If it was for

Chris to serve as an example to the other students, then out of school suspension might serve that purpose.

There did not seem to be any answers. On one occasion the same assistant principal who had suspended Chris called me in frustration. Instead of suspension for misbehavior, he had confined Chris to an office. He left the room temporarily. When he returned he found Chris trying to stick a paper clip in an electric socket!

There were times during the elementary years I did get to enjoy the role of being a parent with a young child. Together we watched movies and television shows that I would have ignored if I did not have a son. The local PBS station would show reruns of *Disney's Wonderful World of Color*. Chris and I both enjoyed "Donald Duck" and "Davy Crockett." Every summer we would go to Rehoboth Beach, Delaware and stay at the SandCastle Motel. Chris loved following the same routine: the first night we would eat at McDonalds, the second pizza, the last would be at a "big people's restaurant." I would take Chris on a regular basis to events at the high school such as athletic contests, dramatic productions, concerts, and science fairs. I hoped to imprint on his mind that these were the things that students did when they were adolescents.

It did not work.

State College

In January of 1995 when Chris was twelve years old, I began working on my PhD in Instructional Systems at Penn State. I would take one course a semester, which would meet one night a week. On our weekly trips Chris and I would leave immediately at the end of the school day and drive the hour and forty-five minutes to State College or the Penn State branch at Great Valley. As I drove Chris would be in the back seat doing homework as I helped him out the best I could. I remember on one occasion he announced, "I need a dictionary!" So we stopped in the Pattee Library at Penn State for a dictionary before heading to class.

Generally there were no problems while I was in class. Chris would sit outside the room and busy himself with his Gameboy. On one occasion he disappeared. I found him in a nearby undergraduate classroom. He was sitting in the back of the room taking notes and pretending to be a student. The undergrads got a kick out of this. On the way back home, Chris would sleep in the backseat, and I would try not to do the same in the front. They were eighteen-hour days.

In August of 1996 we moved to State College, Pennsylvania to do my residency year. We rented our home in Perry County for the year. To get the house ready for the tenants, I had to replace a number of windows and doors. Chris had a habit of destroying both when he got angry. I had found it practical to NOT have them repaired when damaged as Chris was likely to demolish them again.

Before I left for State College, my mother asked how I was going to be a full-time Ph D student, part-time graduate assistant, and full-time father to Chris. I replied that I didn't know. We'd have to go day by day and overcome things as they presented themselves. It might seem amazing to others, but I believe that working on the doctorate actually helped me in raising Christopher. As bad as things would get, I had hope. Someday I would earn my doctorate, and I would have more money and time to help Chris with his problems. That hope would keep me going when things got bad.

The first concern upon moving to State College was getting medication for Chris. Transact had an office in Dubois, Pennsylvania. With the Harrisburg Transact therapist, I went along with a charade that we would stay with that organization, and I would drive to Dubois. Being a 75-minute commute one-way and being strapped for time with my multiple roles, I knew that was not going to happen. Besides, I had given up on talk therapy providing any type of benefit. I decided to go to a physician that was a general practitioner to get a script for meds.

It was a life-altering move. He actually listened to what I had to say about Christopher's problems. He then said that he thought there was "something more here going on than your garden variety ADHD." He recommended that we get a MRI/CT scan. He also asked what Chris was like without meds. I said that I did not know because he had been on medication for many years. So we agreed to try him without medication. Chris was a month shy of the age of fourteen.

One positive outcome of the no-med tryout period was that Chris developed a ravenous appetite. However, there was excessive motor activity. He continuously rammed his head into an easy chair. More noticeably he was oppositional to an extreme. For example, once we were in the grocery story, and I refused to buy something Chris wanted. Chris put the item in the cart anyway. When I placed the item back on the shelf, Chris placed something else, something he did not want, in the cart. In attempt to lighten the situation, I made a face and said, "Isn't this silly?" Chris laughed, but he persisted at this behavior. Additionally, he placed his foot in front of the wheel of the grocery cart to prevent it from moving forward.

Generally the year in State College went well for Chris. He played soccer, and the league was more recreational than competitive, which was a plus for him. He got along with his teammates and coaches. The school was better academically, and had many material advantages. We lived in a community of graduate student families, which were ninety-nine percent international. The first day we moved in, Chris came to me and said, "I told that Mexican kid to keep his hands off my bike." I told him not to create an international incident as we were in the minority.

Chris and I were able to go to many of the athletic events on campus. He particularly enjoyed ice hockey and was able to play the sport himself. For the next few years he would play. Although he was always the worst player on the team, it never seemed to bother him. He enjoyed the camaraderie of being on a team.

On one occasion, when I was away for a weekend and my mother was watching him, he walked the short distance to the hockey arena. He watched the Penn State team play and returned by himself without a problem. He was able to ride the campus bus by himself. In my classes he was a welcome addition. Classes were often long and could last up to three hours. Chris would serve as a gofer for the students and the professors making refreshment runs to the student union.

Other things did not go so well. At the age of fourteen, Chris began to smoke cigarettes, which is something I could not accept. It engendered huge confrontations. I was surprised at the number of people who told me just to let it go that the power struggle was not worth it. All of these people were nonsmokers. My friends that were smokers told me not to give in.

There were still problems related to school. Homework was a constant battle. Often he was unclear as to what his assignments were. About half the days I would drive Chris to school and talk to the teachers directly to get clarification on homework. At home he was resistant to doing it. On one occasion I was so flustered by his obstinacy, I declared that if he did not do the assignment he would have no Nintendo (which he loved) for a month. Chris did not comply, and I put it away without further protest from Chris. Fourteen days later he said, "Two more weeks before Nintendo, right?" I never heard another word about it.

Chris refused to take Physical Education at school. Consequently, he was failing the class although there was no disciplinary action from the school. When I discovered this I told him every time he refused to take Phys Ed, we would run a lap around the track at the IM building on campus in the evening. After the first time we did one lap (260 yards), he was laughing as he finished at the ease of the task. The second time we ran two laps. The third time was three laps, and Chris complained, "This really sucks." I responded, "Yeah, I figure whatever you are doing in Phys Ed has to be more fun than this." It was the last time he refused to take Phys Ed.

In April of 1997 we went to see a Dr. Davis in Lancaster for the MRI/CT scan that the general practitioner in State College had recommended. The findings:

> There is a vague area of diminished density within the left temporal lobe inferiorly. There are no associated calcifications. We did not give enhancement today, since it did not

enhance with gadolinium with the MRI. Again, differential considerations would primarily consist of previous insult to this area of the brain due to either ischemia or possibly trauma. No appreciable mass effect is seen. There are no areas of altered density elsewhere in the brain. The ventricles and subarachnoid spaces are normal. There is no hemorrhage or extra-axial lesion.

IMPRESSION:

A vague area of decreased density involving the inferior left temporal lobe just below the temporal horn. This is probably due to an old insult which may be related to ischemia or trauma.

Translation: Chris's brain had an injury that was very old quite possibly suffered in utero. Dr. Davis said that Chris's mother might have been taking drugs and/or alcohol when she was carrying him.

This stunned me for two reasons. One was because this was the first time, when Chris was fourteen and a half years of age, it had been established there were physiological problems. The second was why no one had bothered to check for this previously. To use an analogy we were always using medication to treat the flow of the liquid through the pipes. But if the pipes were damaged, what good was medication?

Chris 's MRI/CT was followed shortly thereafter with a neuropsychological exam which was a battery of tests. The conclusions:

Chris Rubisch is of mostly average intellectual ability, but has many behaviors indicative of mild prefrontal lobe dysfunction (disinhibition, perseveration, lack of monitoring, sequencing errors, and strategy selection inefficiencies), which can often prevent him from performing adequately and using all his intellectual ability. He attends well in a 1 to 1 setting with constant feedback and wants to do a good job, but he lacks intrinsic motivation for academic pursuits. This is not usually the type of motivation one can increase. Chris sees the world in a more self-centered way and has trouble appreciating what others expect from him especially if it doesn't seem relevant to him. Outside structure and logical consequences are necessary for Chris' compliance. He has deficits in abstract visual-spatial processing, but over time he seems able and motivated to learn visual patterns. He probably has better visual memory than auditory memory. He read adequately but doesn't like to. He is learning disabled in Math and Writing Expression.

When we saw Dr. Davis in Lancaster, he said that there very well could be a problem with the prefrontal lobe although the MRI/CT did not focus on these areas. My understanding is that this area is the "Governance" part of the brain: it decides what to do in interacting with others.

Chris also received a psychological exam in conjunction with the neuropsychological. Its summary and recommendations:

Christopher's Story:
An Indictment Of The American Mental Health System

Summary:

Chris is a fourteen year old boy with a long history of adjustment and learning difficulties, whose current profile suggests significant attentional problems, difficulties with social cognition and reasoning, a focus on fairly short-term temporal awareness of events, with little ability to anticipate or show awareness of the implications for his current behavior. His degree of insight appears to be limited, and many of his personality issues described earlier suggest a more characterological type of pattern, in other words a more stable fairly rigid and inflexible style of coping and adjusting to his external environment.

Recommendations

Continued exploration of medication to address the impulsivity and attentional problems as well as consideration of medication to help with the explosive outbursts should be pursued. I do not feel that Chris is a candidate for individual psychotherapy, rather the level of intervention needs to be more on external structure and behavioral management issues. Chris needs an explicit set of expectations with consequences for violations of these expectations presented to him on a very concrete basis. Similarly, structure in school as well as at home needs to be very consistent with little in the day-to-day routine which would demand much in terms of flexibility for change in coping with additional demands.

Chris finished off his eighth grade year with a failing grade in health, two D-s, three Ds, 2 Cs and two Bs. One of the Bs was in Phys Ed. He attempted to work a job that summer. It lasted two days. He got a new pair of sneakers, which despite my warnings otherwise, he insisted on wearing the next day to work. At work he refused to do the required task, painting, because he did not want to get paint on his new shoes. He was fired.

We returned home to Marysville in August 1997 with the report from Dr. Davis and the results of the neurological workup. With this additional understanding of his problems, I had new hope that we could finally turn things around.

I could not have been more wrong.

Downward Slide

For the first time ever, Chris and I were in the same school building. When my wife and I split up, I intentionally chose a home in the school district in which I worked in the belief I could look out for him. However, my presence in the same building as Chris had a negative effect. Aware that he was my son, some of the teachers were more lenient with his misbehaviors than they would be with other students. Chris quickly developed a reputation among other problem students of being able to flaunt authority and get away with it. He relished this. The administration's response was to punish him more severely than other students. When I questioned the assistant principal about this, he said it had to be shown that Chris received no breaks because his father was on the staff.

Chris visited our local vocational technical school during the fall of 1997 to judge his interest in attending. One of my hopes had always been that he would find his place at Vo-Tech, and this would lead to a successful adjustment into society.

The visit was a disaster. Chris returned fuming. He alleged two students had opened his water bottle in his bookbag and spilled the liquid over the bag's contents. They then said, "Welcome to Vo-Tech." I tried to portray this as some sort of initiation rite and got a teacher to agree. It was no use. Chris never again considered attending the local Vo-Tech.

I was still taking classes for my PhD at Penn State. That fall we were running back and forth for evening classes. In early December on a return trip, Chris became upset when I would not stop at a McDonald's about one-third of the way home. For the next hour he continued to rant and rave. His anger continued once we arrived home. That night he wrote a suicide note:

> *I Chris Rubisch hearby leave all my stuff to (two neighbor boys) cause I'm going to take my life.*
>
> *X Chris Rubisch*

This stunned me as the possibility of Chris committing suicide had never arose. I called a friend, Quinn Zimmerman, and she advised me to take him to an institution near State College at which she had a connection, The Meadows. I took the next day off work, and we drove to The Meadows. To Chris I was evasive about the purpose of our trip other than to say we were going to get him some help. I was unsure as to how he would take being hospitalized. However, while we were waiting to be seen, Chris went outside and bummed a cigarette off a patient. If Chris could smoke at The Meadows, he was all in favor of staying there. He was admitted.

The Meadows

Chris was at The Meadows from December 5 to December 24, 1997. The Meadows is a psychiatric facility. There are locks on the doors and windows. During his stay his behavior was described as follows: impulsive, assaultive, oppositional, defiant, irresponsible, manipulative, non-compliant (in school), and agitated. He was in need of frequent supervision and inclined to anger. Furthermore, he stole from peers and lied to staff as well as peers. He made a superficial suicide attempt (he made slight cuts on his arms). Different medications were tried, but none were successful.

He started to change on December 19, 1997. There was no apparent reason for this improvement and no indication it was anything but a temporary upswing. I met with Dr. King, and I was asked how I felt about Chris returning home. I said I was not sure he was ready. Dr. King suggested that we try it at home. If there were any problems, Chris could return to the Meadows. On Christmas Eve 1997 Chris returned home.

In retrospect the discharge diagnosis could have been illuminating. Chris was diagnosed as having Borderline and Narcissistic Personality Traits. Borderline sounded correct as some of the signs were impulsivity, instability in affect, and frequent displays of anger. Chris was also diagnosed as having Oppositional Defiant Disorder. I always wondered why Chris was never previously diagnosed as ODD as it seemed very apparent to me that he was. My friend David Yates, a professional in the field, said there was reluctance to tag a child with the ODD label as there was no effective treatment. He said the same was true for Borderline and Narcissistic Personality traits. There is no effective treatment.

Although it was there in the report, I cannot say that at that time I could read between the lines. My thought was that Chris was in a hospital. They were going to treat him until he was well. I was skeptical when they talked about returning him home, but I figured to trust in Dr. King particularly with his assurance that Chris could return if things did not go well. They had talked about a RTF (group home), but I could not see this as an option. I thought he was coming home because he was well. If he was not well, The Meadows would have kept him.

When Chris returned home from The Meadows, he went to a partial hospitalization program in Harrisburg also run by The Meadows. He would go there for education and therapy during the day and return home in the mid-afternoon.

At the partial hospitalization program, Chris had frequent peer conflicts. Some escalated to the point of physical aggression. At home things were bad. I started keeping a journal to keep track of everything that happened. At one point during this time period, I do not have the exact date, Chris called the county Children and Youth agency and said I was physically abusing him although nothing like that had occurred.

Journal

February 9, 1998

At age fifteen, despite warnings not to take a knife to school, Chris did. He hid it under the car when I frisked him. Then, he went out and got it. The bus driver found it. The knife had marijuana residue on it. He was angry with Young (a friend) and threatened to get him. Said if he had a gun, he'd blow his head off. Defiant when he got home. Refused to come inside when I told him he must. Stayed outside for about three minutes more. Came in and turned up his music real loud. When I told him to turn it down, he initially did. When I told him to turn it down lower, he got mad and blasted it. I shut it down. He then went upstairs and destroyed his radio/tape player. Later that night he asked what was going to happen to him. He said he was afraid that he would go to jail. He said that this is why he acted agitated when told that he was grounded.

February 14, 1998

Found a lighter in Christopher's pocket. When I took it away from him, he got mad and kicked a hole in the hall door. He got this lighter from kids who came by the house.

February 25, 1998

I tried to talk Chris into attending a ski club event. He locked himself in his room and refused to go. Initially, I tried to physically pull him off the bed. When I gave up he went outside in the yard. I told him that he had to go inside, and he refused. I told him that he could pack his bags to stay at The Meadows. He went inside and packed a suitcase. He was still quite agitated. I told him to stay in the house and that we should avoid each other. I also told him that I had to be at the school at

6PM. When I checked on him a half hour later, he was gone. Did not return by 5:50, so I left for school and locked the door. When I returned at 9:10, he was in the house, having climbed in a window. There was a smell in the air, and he said he and a friend had been burning incense. He was calmed down and apologized (unusual), but said it was partly my fault. He said he walked out of the house to keep from destroying things. He did rip the arm off a stuffed animal, Parrot, which he closely associates with me.

February 26, 1998

When I told Chris his punishment for yesterday would be grounding for a week, he asked if it could start tomorrow instead of today. When I said it couldn't, he got agitated and said he would go out anyway. Then, as we pulled into the school parking lot where he would catch the bus to go to the partial program, he asked me to escort him to the teacher's lounge to use the vending machines (he couldn't enter without me). I pointed out the contradiction in his recent behavior: being defiant but wanting favors. He got out of the car and yelled in the parking lot so everyone could hear "Lick my balls."

February 27, 1998

I found out that Chris was smoking marijuana and engaged in vandalism when I was at school the evening of the 25th.

Christopher's Story:
An Indictment Of The American Mental Health System

March 2, 1998

Chris was still grounded from last week. I had to go to the school to pick something up. He refused to go with me even when I told him he would be grounded for another week. When I returned in fifteen minutes, he was with another kid in the yard. I told the kid to leave, and he did without a problem. However, Chris went with him. I went racing after Chris. He refused to come home. I struggled with him trying to pull him back. He was screaming and yelling all the way. He bent both my middle fingers back and was close to breaking them. I let him go. A neighbor saw what happened and threatened to harm me. Chris called the police and said he was being abused. The officer sided with me when he found out Chris was grounded for taking drugs and engaging in vandalism. Chris was in tears and very apologetic.

End of Journal

From the Notes of The Meadows Outpatient Psychiatric Program in Harrisburg:

By March 4, 1998, it was the decision of the entire Treatment Team that this patient's behavior was creating a risky situation to himself and to his father. He had recently been informed that the plans were in place to pursue Residential Treatment Facility placement and this was creating additional stress in the father

and son relationship. A decision was made at
that time to pursue inpatient psychiatric
hospitalization.

That is not how I remember it. Chris was out of my
control. Previously, if worse came to worst, I could always
physically restrain him. At the age of fifteen, I could no longer
do that. Additionally, I had a neighbor threatening to do me
bodily harm; a neighbor who Chris had run to when he did not
want to obey me. I had no alternative but to have him replaced
at The Meadows.

However, the intake worker at The Meadows did not see it
that way. It did not matter what I said; it was dismissed or
discounted. Bringing the knife to school? He did not see it as
serious. Use of illicit drugs? No big deal. Could not control
him? There were homes where parents were specially trained to
deal with problem children. This caught my attention. Perhaps
it was time to swallow my pride if there were others out there
that could help my son. I asked for more information and
learned he was talking about putting Chris in a Children and
Youth foster home.

I was ready to explode. I knew foster parents because I had
worked with them. They had nothing to offer that I could not
provide. I then knew I was being deliberately diverted from
having my son admitted. I told him that Dr. King had said to
bring Chris back if there were any problems. He responded that
there was nothing written on the discharge papers from
December to that effect. Angrily I demanded that he call Dr.
King.

He picked up the phone and dialed someone. When he got
off the phone he said, "If it is not written down, it is not written
down."

Christopher's Story:
An Indictment Of The American Mental Health System

I was stunned. I thought about picking up his letter opener and slitting my wrist. They were going to take one of us, because the two of us together was not going to work. Instead, I called my friend Quinn Zimmerman who had a connection to The Meadows as a part-time employee. She called someone. Shortly afterward the intake worker told me Chris would be admitted.

Afterwards, I talked to my friend David Yates. He had extensive experience in the mental health field. He told me that my medical insurance had paid for Chris's placement in December when he was placed for the first time at The Meadows. But when we went back in March, the medical insurance had been exhausted. Consequently, The Meadows would have to bill the Pennsylvania Department of Welfare for his care. Welfare would pay them at a lower rate than private insurance. The Meadows preferred to save the space for a patient with private insurance as they would receive more money. He said this was the reason for the run-around at the intake meeting.

Once he was back in psychiatric placement at The Meadows, Chris did not improve. In his initial interview, when asked why he was at The Meadows, he responded, "Ask my father." When asked why he was angry, he said, "Because I'm sitting here talking to you. I'd rather be sleeping."

Chris was in psychiatric placement from March 4, 1998 to April 15, 1998. His behavior during this time period was described as superficial, oppositional, defiant, disrespectful, impulsive, and unpredictable. It was decided in mid-April that Chris would be transferred to a Residential Treatment Facility (group home). The RTF was also at The Meadows. Dr. King ruled out a return home as he could be dangerous to himself or me. You will note that Chris's behavior for March and April was essentially the same as it had been prior to placement. Yet, his placement was downgraded from psychiatric to RTF.

Chris did not markedly improve at the RTF. In June Chris became enraged when a peer tried to upset a chair on which Chris was resting his feet. Knocking the chair over Chris grabbed the boy by the neck. When staff tried to intervene, he yelled, "I swear that I'll hurt him if you come near me and that is not a threat, that's a promise." Chris was placed in a saferoom where he pounded the walls with his fists and banged his head. Chris was temporarily transferred back to the Adolescent Intensive Care Unit.

There was a CASSP (Child and Adolescent Service System Program) meeting on November 4, 1998 during which there was a recommendation for Chris to go to Crossroads, a group home. Participating in the program were Virginia Diaz, Thomas Miller of The Meadows, Yaden Nelson of Holy Spirit Community Health Center, Chris and me.

Supposedly Chris was getting better. But I always had the impression The Meadows was looking to get rid of him ASAP. I remember thinking they would have released him to a garbage can in a back alley of Philadelphia if I had let them. Here is his track record for his last months at The Meadows RTF. Judge for yourself:

➢ September 1998- lost two of four weekend passes because of behavior
➢ October 19, 1998- dropped level for fighting
➢ October 20, 1998- screaming and swearing in group because "tired of this place"
➢ October 29, 1998- stormed out of his therapy group with Dr. Vasquez and was yelling "fuck you" and showed Dr. Vasquez his middle finger

Christopher's Story:
An Indictment Of The American Mental Health System

- November 2, 1998- lost level for not doing homework
- November 8, 1998- horseplay lost level
- November 10, 1998- lost level for not doing homework
- November 15, 1998- lost level for punching a peer
- November 27, 1998- ninety minute snit over Pepsi
- November 28, 1998- sexual intercourse with girl
- December 3, 1998- lost level for kissing girl
- December 8, 1998- lost level for being in girl's lav with girl, he said his only problem was everyone at The Meadows
- December 11, 1998- in fist fight with roommate
- December 26, 1998- got into grandfather's Scotch on Christmas visit
- January 11, 1999- lost level, did not do homework
- January 14, 1999- lost level
- January 18, 1999- on shutdown

Dr. Yoder's amazing conclusion on Chris's discharge in February 1999: Chris had shown improvement in his ability to manage his thoughts, feelings and behaviors.

Many years later Chris told me that after he had the sexual intercourse with the girl, Dr. Yoder said The Meadows was going to move him out. And they did.

Just prior to his discharge from The Meadows, in December 1998 and January 1999, Chris was seen by Dr. Kevin Vargas at the Hershey Medical Center. Vargas is a nationally renowned expert in the brain. His findings:

Chris scored high on lack of planning, lack of flexibility, emotionality, and aggressiveness. Surprisingly, he scored in the midrange of impulsiveness. He scored low in the following areas: excess caution, attention, memory, arousal level, social monitoring, and empathy.

He said the damage in Chris's brain was the size of a golf ball. The damage was in the limbic system. The limbic system connects with the prefrontal lobe. The limbic regulates emotion. When damaged the brain may not develop as quickly as it should. However, it could still develop as he matured.

Crossroads

The evaluation by Dr. Vargas did not change the plans of The Meadows. Chris was discharged to the Crossroads group home in Mt. Gretna, PA. on February 1, 1999. Philhaven of Mt. Gretna, Pa ran Crossroads. Chris lived in an old farmhouse with supervisory adults and other adolescent boys with mental health problems. The number of boys would vary, but it would always be in single digits. He attended a public high school and was in a room for special education students with emotional problems. Crossroads used a level system. If Chris did well, his level would go up, and he would be able to come home weekends on a pass. If he misbehaved, his level would go down, and he would lose his weekend pass. Many times Chris did not have the level needed to come home on weekends

Journal

March 25, 1999

Lost weekend pass. Punched boy in the group home. Swearing and out of control. Staff afraid. Placed at Philhaven (lockup, psychiatric) for weekend. He lost a weekend pass to see cousin act in play, go out to eat with grandmother, go to state championship basketball game. All of these were very important to him.

May 16, 1999

Chris is home for the weekend. He is up early at 7 AM. Nancy Sanchez, my girlfriend, complains twice about loud noise from him playing the TV and stereo. After church, Larry Scott, Chris's best friend (and more importantly, one that I approve of), is here for the afternoon. Chris is antsy. Wants to walk around town, but Larry doesn't want to do so. Chris wants to go to movie, but I said no. We have to have him at home to see how it goes. Rented two movies. Then Chris wants to go to a coffee shop in Annville. I say yes but only on our way back. When we get to Crossroads, I find my portable TV hidden in Chris's stuff. His excuse is "You don't use it anyway."

July 23, 1999

Chris was dropped to Red level (the lowest) the night before for having a lighter and matches. Smelled like smoke. Was supposed to go on weekend pass, see friend Larry Scott, go to Big 33 Football Game. Lost his pass. I told him on the phone he needed to apologize to Larry and that he had let him and me down. He called back and said that he didn't want to see me on Sunday. When I asked, he acknowledged that he shouldn't be mad at me. But still didn't want to see me Sunday, the 25th.

Christopher's Story:
An Indictment Of The American Mental Health System

August 6- 8, 1999

Good weekend with Chris. Was home Friday and Saturday night. Went to Inner Harbor in Baltimore on Saturday the 7th.

August 15, 1999

Good weekend visit with Chris. Went to Knoebels Grove amusement park.

September 1, 1999

Since last notation Chris has dropped to Green (one level drop) at least once and perhaps twice. One was for sitting on a kid's head in the van when the kid would not give Chris the front seat. Today was not a good day for Chris. Talked to his new teacher. Chris did not want to be on a point system. Said to just give him detention if he misbehaved. Also, said that he did not have to do his homework if he did not want to do so. Got a call from Evelyn (therapist at Crossroads) in the evening. Chris was on Red. Got very angry. It was all verbal. He was in a bad mood last night about not being able to go to the mall. Still in a bad mood this PM when he found a boy he doesn't like in his room. Evelyn promised to talk to Chris but forgot to do so. Got Chris to come into group where he vented. He was very angry, beyond proper bounds. Went off on Evelyn in group and later on after group. She was very surprised. I said at least he did not get physical. Other staff members said it was like the old Chris. She said she had never seen him that way.

September 9, 1999

Not a good week for Chris. On Red again today. Many problems at school. Work not getting done. He disappeared from the school. He said he went outside of the building. Teacher gave him chance to do Algebra in class, and he didn't. Chris wants to drop German and Algebra. Claims that he can't get work done at Crossroads as there is too much noise, too many chores to do. When I talked to Evelyn it was clear that Chris was doing what he had done in the past: procrastinate. Evelyn says he is lazy and does not want to do homework nor chores. Chris said he was being oppositional defiant at school. We set up a meeting for Tuesday September 14. Chris says he will not show up as Evelyn and I will decide, and he won't have a voice. He is objecting to the implementation of a point system at school.

September 14, 1999

Chris was out of control when I arrived at school. Teacher suspects that he was sneaking out to a parked car and smoking during the school day. When I arrived, he was waiting out in the parking lot for me. He was refusing to come in for the meeting. Evelyn told him no McDonalds with me if he didn't come to the meeting. He would have to go home with her.

He came in and ranted and raved for 20 minutes about how much he hated Palmyra High School. One cannot reason with Chris when he is like this. I successfully distracted him by telling the teacher a story about Chris from the previous day. On that day I said to Chris if Cameron Diaz showed up in a bikini and wanted to go on a date with Chris, and I wanted Chris to go, Chris would refuse just because I wanted him to do so. The same thing would happen if someone offered him a million dollars, and I told him to take it. Chris laughed at the recounting of this tale, and his whole demeanor changed so that we could talk with him. We dropped German, and he will take US History (Civil War) in special needs in its place. He will stay with Algebra. The rest of the afternoon went fine.

September 25, 1999

Chris on Red. Engaged in horseplay with another boy. It got out of hand, and Chris punched the boy in the nose and drew blood. He would have been taken to Philhaven psychiatric except that there was not room there.

February 6, 2000

Chris on Red. Shoving match over use of bathtub.

<u>End of Journal</u>

While Chris was at Crossroads, I was continuously looking for new placement facilities for him. I would even go to the extent of visiting them. This is not something usually done by a parent. However, my experience with the mental health system, particularly with The Meadows, had taught me that the system could not be trusted to return Chris only after he had made sufficient therapeutic process. The staff of Crossroads found out about my research and assured me that Chris would remain there as long as he was in need.

Chris was doing well in the early part of the summer of 2000. It looked like he might earn his way home. However, his behavior began to deteriorate in August. He had a part-time job at a local grocery store. He was fired for allegedly urinating on the shopping carts. He denied doing so. However, it sounded like something he would do.

Chris started his senior year in Fall 2000. At one time I had hoped that Chris would take five years to complete four years of high school. Not that he necessarily would fail courses. However, an extra year in school, given his lack of maturity, could not hurt.

I had discarded that idea by Fall 2000 as it was apparent it would be all we could do to get him through his last year. Chris, like many youths, attached a magical significance to his eighteenth birthday. He would be eighteen! An adult! No one could tell him what to do! He had talked to me about this, but I placed no special significance to it. He turned eighteen on October 23. On November 6, a Monday, he went to school and never returned to Crossroads.

Eventually, Chris did call. He ended up at the home of a religious zealot in the Lebanon area. Then he moved to my brother's home, which was also in Lebanon. Chris wanted to return home, but I refused. I maintained that he still needed help, and he was to return to the Crossroads group home which he refused to do. Ultimately we reached a compromise of getting Chris a room in Lebanon. I bought him a microwave and a small refrigerator. He was to get a job. When I offered to buy him a bike to get to the yet unknown job, he said he did not need one. He would commute via skateboard (too much Michael J. Fox in *Back to the Future*). It didn't matter. In less than a week, Chris was thrown out of the room. In doing so he lost the microwave and the refrigerator.

Shortly thereafter I got a call from Chris one evening. He was crying. He had had a run in with a Latino street gang. He was scared and wanted to come home.

At this point I still believed that Chris needed to be in a therapeutic setting like Crossroads. On the other hand, if anything might make a difference in him, it might have been this encounter with the gang. I agreed to him returning home, and he did so on December 15 of 2000. Did I think it was going to work? No. But I felt I had to give it one more chance.

Last Chance

There was a short honeymoon period when Chris first returned home at the end of 2000. On January 18 of 2001, I started keeping a journal of events. This is a sure indication things were on a downward slide. The next five months were an avalanche of theft, substance abuse, explosive emotional outbursts in school and community, inappropriate sexual advances toward girls that were too young for him, and an unresponsive and callous mental health system. In the early months of 2001, I felt like I was walking on a razor's edge. I was always trying to anticipate what he might do next. Sometimes I did. But at other times there was nothing I could do.

<u>Journal</u>

January 18, 2001

Chris came back fifteen minutes late for curfew. He said the police had stopped and questioned him about the vandalization of a laundromat that had occurred a few days ago. Chris told me he did it while engaged in horseplay. He must have been in a confessional mood. He told me he had used my credit card number to subscribe to some internet porn sites. We sent them e-mails to take care of it. He wanted to sleep in front of the TV. I initially said no. But he promised there would be no problems getting up in the morning and told me to take my wallet to bed. I agreed, but also said that I would take the phone off the hook in my room (this would break the chance to connect to the net). I woke up shortly before midnight and found Chris in my room. He said he needed a sleeping pill as he couldn't fall asleep. I gave it to him. I then heard him talking downstairs. He had placed the phone back on the hook when he entered my room. I picked it up and heard him trying to make a transaction to buy CDs. He had copied my credit card number on a piece of paper. He had known this when he told me to take my wallet to bed.

January 19, 2001

Chris failed on his promise to get out of bed right away even though he had two extra hours of sleep due to a weather delay. When he wouldn't get out of bed, I started to pull him out. He started to swear at me, and I slapped him on the cheek. He got out of bed and started to rage. I went to the phone and called 911. He yanked the phone out of the wall. When the police called back, he hung up on another phone. He pushed me. Later on that day he said he would have hit me with a baseball bat if he had one. When he understood the police would be coming, he calmed down and asked me to call them off. The state police took about thirty minutes to arrive from Newport. Things were calm by then. They took my side. I called Harold Garcia, Virginia Diaz, MHMR intake, and saw Ian Ingram (same person we had seen years ago for counseling) in the hallway at school and got to talk to none of them. Not one person returned my calls. Eventually, George Peterson (of Susquenita) got a hold of Virginia Diaz, and I talked to her. Really didn't get too far. She said she had called me four times at home but left no messages. Then why was there no indication that she called on caller ID? She did fax me some papers to set up a CASSP meeting. Also, faxed some stuff about wraparounds.

(A wraparound is an adult that follows a troubled student around school. The adult is supposed to be Jiminy Cricket on his shoulder. This was a typical MH lowball response. We were way past the wrap around stage by this point).

We went to the Marysville police, and Chris confessed to vandalizing a laundromat. It happened a little over a week ago. The police knew another neighborhood kid was in on it but were less sure about Chris. There would be charges pressed. Chris was fined $241.50 for this. Police officer Quentin Hernandez said I could get a domestic restraint even for verbal abuse. I told Chris that the next time he used my credit card I would press charges. I made up rules and restrictions, which he seemed to accept.

End of Journal

Chris's return to Susquenita High School in January, where I worked, was a disaster. He refused to do his work, was impulsive, and emotionally reactive with students and teachers.

To make matters worse his movement from the Crossroads group home to the streets of Lebanon to home had disrupted his medication treatment. I had called Holy Spirit. The best they could do was tell me that we could be seen in mid-March. They could not even give me a specific date.

<u>Journal</u>

January 31. 2001

    Early this morning before going to school, Chris had a tantrum. His storage towers for CDs fell over accidently. Chris got mad and sent CDs flying everywhere. After going to school Chris became further agitated by a kid named Victor who had taunted him about the vandalism at the laundromat. He told a teacher that he was concerned he would hit this kid if he saw him again in in-school suspension (Chris had been placed there for misbehavior). The teacher told the assistant principal who asked me to take him home. I suggested that we call Holy Spirit. We did and got an appointment for 1:30 with Ian Ingram, the same therapist we had seen years ago. Ingram worked with the high school as part of the Teenline Program. I was asked about medication. I told them about our difficulty in scheduling an appointment. Although I had sent information on Chris to Holy Spirit a week ago, we had yet to hear from them. Chris talked to Ingram for a little over an hour. Ingram said he thought Chris had a dual diagnosis of mental health and drug and alcohol, and he would refer us to Nicole Harris of Perry Human Services for a drug and alcohol evaluation. We tried to reach her by phone, but she was not available. Ingram said Chris was a medium to high threat in school. He would pass this on to the principals of Susquenita. In his opinion they would likely suspend Chris from school. I told him of what had happened with Chris and the credit cards and said that he could not be trusted alone at home. Ingram suggested that I stay at home with Chris. I strongly objected stating I had responsibilities at work. I also stated that I would be enabling the mental health system to get away with its dysfunctional behavior. As long as I baby-sat Chris, there would be no need for intervention on their part. We argued about this for perhaps an hour. Chris and I were in favor of Chris being placed in some type of mental health facility. Ingram refused to consider this. He finally said that he had to go. I asked for someone else to take over. After checking, Ingram said that they were busy with two emergency admittances, it would take a few hours for them to get to us, and when they did, the process would have to start all over again. Talk about getting blown off! We left.

Afterwards, I asked Chris what he told Ingram as far as drug and alcohol use. He said he told him that he smoked cigarettes and drank a lot of soda, nothing more. Granted that Chris could be less than honest, but on this occasion, I sensed that he was telling the truth (at least about what he said). And it was more than just a hunch. I had worked with Ingram as part of the Student Assistance Program, a statewide program for troubled students. When students were referred with problems that required outside intervention, Ingram, in 99% of the cases, would say that he thought there should be a drug and alcohol (D&A) evaluation first before the case would go to himself and mental health.

Sometime later I obtained Holy Spirit's notes from January 31. Ingram's recommendation was for a drug and alcohol evaluation and to file our info until further contact! Not only were we unable to get a placement, Ingram was unwilling to assist us in getting an appointment with the psychiatrist.

February 2, 2001

Due to his suspension Chris was not in school, and since I could not trust him alone, he stayed with the same sitter he had as a young boy. There was a meeting to talk about the suspension and what to do with him. It was decided his disability did have a large effect on his behavior that resulted in the suspension. I said I wanted an alternative to Susquenita, and George Peterson gave me a phone number to set it up an appointment to visit a school for students with behavioral problems. As Ian Ingram predicted Principal Evans said Chris would be suspended from school even though he had maxed out his dates for the year (there is a limit to the number of days a special education student can be suspended). I said I was going to be very pragmatic with Chris's situation. I would not fight the suspension at this time because I thought it was in his best interest. However, if matters changed, I might change my mind as well. Mr. Flores (teacher) said that Chris was making the threats sufficiently loud on January 31 that everyone in the classroom could hear it. When I got home Chris had failed to do any of his chores. I told him if he did not complete his chores, he would be unable to play in his hockey game. He completed the chores quickly.

February 3, 2001

Chris slept until about 11 AM (it was a Saturday). When we went to the Giant grocery store, I found that my bank account was short of what I thought it would be. Turns out there had been some more calls to porn sites on January 18. One of the bills alone was for $800! These charges had not been on the last statement. I figured out the mortgage check had yet to be received by the company. When it did on Monday (February 5), I wouldn't have enough money to pay for it! I called and got the porn charges straightened out.

February 6, 2001

The sitter was unable to watch Chris on this morning. Before I left for school, he was acting suspicious, and I deduced that something was up. I came home at 10 AM to find eighteen-year old Chris alone with a thirteen-year-old girl. There were no signs of sexual activity. Not able to take him to school as he was suspended and not wanting to leave him home, I left him off at the diner in a remote area for a ninety-minute breakfast. In the PM we checked out an alternative education program, which did not interest him. Talked to Ian Ingram. He tried to talk to Chris as well but could not reach him at home. I told Ingram that after a week from the original crisis we've had two more crises (bank and the 13 year old girl), had to place Chris at a diner as MH was unwilling to place him in an appropriate setting, and we had yet to get an appointment with the psychiatrist.

February 16, 2001

At about 3:30 AM Chris woke me up and said that he was freezing. I took his temperature, and it was 94! He took a hot shower and switched into my sweats. When he awoke in the morning, he said something about staying home. This was a very bad idea as Susquenita students would be off the day for an in-service day, and I would have to be at the in-service. That would leave Chris at home free to find trouble with the riff-raff in town. I told him I would have to call in sick if he was sick. Saying that he wouldn't do any work, he went reluctantly to Wordsworth (he had started in this alternative school on the fourteenth), which was in session for the day. He ended up in in-school suspension at Wordsworth and said he would not go back. When I was doing the wash that evening, I went through his pockets and found a note from Norma. Apparently written the day before, she asked Chris to sneak out of the house at 12:30 and meet her in the woods. She also said she was high while writing the note, and it made her horny! When I confronted him with the note, Chris said he hadn't actually gone out. I told him nevertheless, he was going to have to sleep with his door open and his music very low in order that I could hear him if he tried to go out. Some weeks later I found something he wrote about this day. He had snuck out in the middle of the night and was making out with the girl in a wooded section near our house. It was cold and rainy.

February 18, 2001

I got a call mid-afternoon from a woman with the last name of Ulrich. She said that Chris was at her home threatening her thirteen-year-old son. When she found out that Chris was eighteen, she said she was going to press charges. A state policeman showed up at my door at 5 PM. Chris had been to the Ulrich house a total of three times and had almost gotten into a fight with the boy's father. Allegedly he was doing this for Norma. The boy was her ex-boyfriend. The officer and I went looking for Chris. We found him with

Harry (someone he's not supposed to be with). The officer talked to Chris. I grounded Chris for a week.

February 25, 2001 (this was a Sunday)

This evening Chris went off. He was ranting about Natalie, her mother, and her brother. Her mother had told Natalie that she could no longer see Chris. Her brother had threatened Chris a few days ago. Chris talked to Natalie on the phone. Then he left briefly to go to the neighborhood store. Perhaps he went to Natalie's house as it is in the same direction. He returned home and continued his rant. It was about 9:30 PM. Initially, he said that he wanted to walk around all night to vent his anger, and he would be back in time in the AM to go to school. When I said no he kept after me. He said this was the only way to handle his anger. Otherwise, he would be down at Natalie's house banging on her door. I suggested alternatives: find another person to deliver his notes to her, or watch James Bond on TV with me. I told him that I loved him and tried to hug him. He let me do this for a while. I brought up his cousin for whom he has a soft spot. I suggested alternatives to walking around town: walk up and down the alley, walk out front of the house, or walk with me. But he would accept none of these. He just got angrier. He turned it on me and said if he had a baseball bat he would hit me with it. I didn't buy into the anger. As he was on restriction, he wanted my approval to leave the house. I said I wouldn't give him my blessing to leave; neither did I say that he couldn't. At 10 PM I went to bed as I usually do. Chris left the house. He returned at 12:30 AM and wanted to continue the tirade. I said I was too tired. He said he would not go to school the next day lest he get into a fight with someone. Furthermore, he said if I was going to throw him out of the house for fighting at school, to go ahead and do so. I went back to sleep. The next day Chris was resistant to going to school, but he did make it.

End of Journal

How did I handle Chris's downward slide? I felt powerless to stop it. There was always this feeling in the back of my mind that this could not be happening to me that I must be in a bad dream. I tried to respond rationally and not let panic or emotions overcome me. Chris was always on a short fuse. It was not going to be helpful to have both of us driven by anger. Most, but not all of the time, I was able to keep myself under control. I attempted to discipline Chris through the use of groundings or extra chores. This had mixed results. He did start talk therapy in February of 2001. It had neither a positive or negative effect.

On March 5 I grounded him when I overheard him trying to make a drug deal on the phone. He left the house and did return home that evening. For the next few days, I was not for sure where he was during the day. He was sneaking into the house in the middle of the night through the basement window. He eventually returned home. I began to lock the windows to ensure this did not happen again. A month later he smashed one of the windows to get in.

Journal

March 14, 2001

> We finally got to see the psychiatrist. We talked to Dr. Yang for about one hour and forty-five minutes. This is a long time with a psychiatrist. Although he said nothing definite, he said the prognosis was not good. He did talk about a wraparound or residential placement.

End of Journal

Chris's ventures into the world of drugs were beginning to violate the sanctuary of my home. I have always believed in separating my school life from my personal life. One night while working on my computer, I looked up to see a young man standing next to me. I knew from school that he was involved with drugs. He was very polite, but just seeing him in my home shocked and disturbed me. Chris was nowhere around. The boy left shortly thereafter.

Journal

April 4, 2001

> Young, a friend of Chris, awakened us at 12:30 AM. Young appeared to be drunk. He had difficulty standing. He said his seventeen-year-old brother was at home and was talking about committing suicide. He said he had

knives. Chris wanted to walk with Young up to Young's house. When I told Chris I would call the police if he left the house, Chris went off and called me every name imaginable. Young told Chris not to leave. He said if the police showed up it would only make matters worse.

Eventually, they called and found out the brother had gone to sleep. Chris wanted to accompany Young up to talk to his mother. I permitted him to do so. They didn't get back to go to bed until 3:45 AM! Young told me to awaken him at 6 AM to go to school. I was unable get him up. I noticed an empty beer bottle in the room. Neither Chris nor Young went to school. When I confronted Chris about the beer, he said he gave it to Young to settle him down. He also acknowledged drinking it and said that they had drunk vodka as well. When I talked about grounding him, he got very belligerent. He called me a dickhead among other things. He said he was too old to be grounded. Then, he did an insulting imitation of a deaf person in which he mumbled with a stupid look on his face. Simultaneously he waggled his fingers near his mouth as if he was using sign language. I grabbed him and told him to leave. Of course, he did not. We cooled down and settled on no music for a week. This was acceptable to me as I hated his music. If I grounded him he would be around me the rest of the evening. I felt that was asking for trouble. Chris went to sleep with the door locked which concerned me as he had a lit candle in his room.

<u>End of Journal</u>

As Chris and free time in the community was a bad mix, I attempted to resolve this problem by getting him a part-time job. As might be expected he was less than enthusiastic about working. But I drove him around, and he filled out applications. Eventually, he did get a job at Wendy's

<u>Journal</u>

April 5, 2001

The police showed up at the door at about 9:30 PM. Chris is their main suspect for something that happened just past midnight. Someone was going through unlocked cars stealing stuff. When I got Chris back from Wendy's, they talked to him. Chris volunteered to show him his room so that they could see he wasn't hiding any stuff in it. The cops seemed unconvinced. Eventually, Chris was cleared of the thefts.

April 6, 2001

When I got home this afternoon, Chris said that he did not want to go to work. While we were arguing about this, his boss called. She offered to start him two hours later. He would start at 7 PM instead of 5. He agreed with this, and I took him to the job. But he called at about 9:15 and wanted to quit. I told him to try to work it out. He called at about a half hour later and said he walked off the job. There did not seem to be any precipitating event. He just did not want to be there.

I discovered tonight that my cell phone was missing from the car. Presumably it was stolen the other night, the incident for which Chris was the main suspect. I called in and got my service canceled. When Chris found this out, he was angry: people trying to smear his name with something he didn't do. I told him he was not permitted out when he returned from Wendy's (about 10:30 PM), but he went out anyway looking for the kids who broke into the cars.

April 11, 2001

Today we had an appointment to get the results from our meeting with the psychiatrist in March. Dr. Yang, the psychiatrist, called about midday to see if we could come in earlier for our appointment that day. I arranged to do so. When I got to Wordsworth, two of Chris's teachers wanted to talk to me. He is doing nothing academically, sleeps in class, does not participate in Phys Ed, and is not meeting the requirements of his IEP. Chris was ticked off because I picked him up. His practice is to leave his cell phone on the van when left off for school in the morning. As I was picking him up, he would be without his phone for the long Easter vacation (until April 17). We were arguing in the car on the way to the appointment. I was trying to confront him about his lack of effort. He called me a dickhead and threatened to physically harm me. When we got to the psychiatrist's, Chris refused to come in. I went in, and Dr. Yang gave me his findings. They were the result of our consultation in March and the reading of Chris's past records. He found Chris to have severe Oppositional Defiant Disorder, and Antisocial Personality Disorder with traits in the borderline and narcissistic areas. Translation into English is that Chris was in really bad shape. These disorders are difficult to treat. He gave him a GAF (Global Assessment of Functioning) score of 45/50. On this scale 100 is high and means an individual is highly adaptive to life. Zero is low. Forty-five to fifty is one step above delusional. His recommendation was long-term psychoanalytic counseling (think Freud), but he was not optimistic about its chances for success.

Amazingly, Dr. Yang's conclusions did not suggest placement or even medication but merely a wrap-around! I said from my perspective we had nothing to lose by trying medication. If untreated Chris was going to end up dead or in prison. Dr. Yang agreed, but said he couldn't prescribe anything unless Chris came in. I got Chris to come in by promising I would call about his phone while he talked to the psychiatrist. We got a prescription for Prozac and Trazodone. When we got home Chris was still fuming about his phone. He broke the glass in the storm window with the palm of his hand. We finally got the phone, and there were no other problems.

End of Journal

The negligence of the MH system during the first five months of 2001 staggered belief. Already cited was the encounter with Ian Ingram on January 31, and Dr. Yang's psychiatric evaluation. Additionally, there was Harold Garcia who I called on January 19, April 17, and May 1. He never returned a call. But no one could top Virginia Diaz. I called her on January 19, April 16, April 17, April 20, April 24, and April 27 and NEVER got a return call. The only time I talked to her was on January 19 when a colleague reached her by phone and transferred the call. I was beyond frustrated with the perpetual dysfunction of the system.

Journal

April 24, 2001

I got a call from the nurse at Wordsworth today. Chris was acting like he was comatose at school. He would freeze while in the act of writing something on his paper. It was an act. He was very upset when I got home from school this afternoon. Someone had called on his cell phone and left a threatening message. It was very explicit. The guy said that he would kill Chris. Chris was extremely agitated. He called Zelma Dixon (his girlfriend). Evidently it was a friend of hers. She and/or her sister called back eight times that afternoon. Chris got more agitated after each call. I finally took the phone and asked them to quit calling. She said she wanted her stuff back from Chris, and I said that we could do it over the weekend (today was a Tuesday). Chris was upset that the police were not responding quickly to our report of the threat. He said that he would call them up and threaten them (the police), and they would be sure to get to our house! The police showed up shortly thereafter before Chris phoned in his threat. The officer told me there was little they could do. Early in the evening I got a call from a woman who lives three blocks up the street. She said Chris had tried to get her twelve-year-old daughter to have sex with him. She also had in her possession an e-mail that Chris had sent her daughter. She said the language was unbelievably profane. I asked her to send me a copy. The e-mail had my name on it because Chris had used my email address! I fought off the panic that arose in me as I thought of the possibility of losing my job or being incarcerated. I calmly told her that Chris had sent the email, and I would take care of it. She said she understood and considered the matter over. Earlier, as Virginia Diaz was not in (so what else is new?), I had talked to Helen Stewart of Holy Spirit. Told her of my problems in setting up a CASSP meeting to discuss Chris's problems. She said she would

get back to me on April 27. There was no
return call from Stewart on the 27th.

April 25, 2001

I got a hold of the Stevens Center in
Carlisle about residential services. Talked to
Heather York, Chris's caseworker, about
placement of Chris in residential services. It is
similar to assisted living. She had to refer him.
She said that she has 700 people on her
caseload!

April 30, 2001

Chris did not go to school today. That was
not a surprise considering that he got home
after midnight last night. I got a call from
Gloria Underwood's parents. He had showed
up there last night. To Gloria, he made a
threatening remark to kill her mother. He also
said that he would make her brother "eat
curb." I had left a message for Chris this
morning that he was to be home at 2:30 PM to
go to the therapist or that I would cut off his
phone service. When we got to the therapist,
Chris did a lot of talking. He called me a
dickhead, among other things. He wanted to
live in a nearby town, Duncannon. He said he
would not finish school. As far as making a
living, he said he would get his friends to drive
him to work. I countered with helping him
find a place in Carlisle. He said he didn't want
to live there. I told him I wanted his keys if he
moved out. If he broke a window to get into

the house, I would call the police. I said I was considering calling the police anyway in light of what happened on April 27 when he stole $30 from me. When we went to leave the appointment with the therapist, he expected to get in the car. I said the only way he was getting in the car was if I got his keys. He threw them at me. On the way back he was trying to make all kinds of deals with me. I said no. He is grounded until a week from today, no phone, and chores for lunch money.

<u>End of Journal</u>

As May began, I hoped to get Chris to graduation which was a little over a month away. Then, he could hopefully move to assisted living with mental health. If that did not work out, my backup plan was to find him an apartment and pay for the first two months of rent and utilities with his grandfather's trust fund (my father had set up a trust fund for each of his grandchildren to go to college). After two months he would be responsible for his expenses. I hoped that this would force him into getting a job. Chris had said he had a plan to sell drugs at a lower price than other people. I told him he would be dead.

<u>Journal</u>

May 3, 2001

I got a call about 8:30 today saying that Chris had arrived at school drunk. He had been drinking Mike's Hard Lemonade. While driving to Wordsworth to pick him up, I had second thoughts. I stopped and called

Wordsworth and told them to call the police. When I got to the police station shortly after three to pick him up, they had already released him! I went home, and he arrived shortly thereafter. He said, "I guess you are going to throw me out." I said no, but there would be new restrictions: indefinite grounding, only one phone call a night of ten minute duration, allowed to smoke once an hour, on the hour, for ten minutes. He said he wasn't going to live with that. I told him he could leave and if he broke in, I would call the police. He started to lose it calling me names. I went upstairs to grab my money before I went out jogging. In the short time that he had been home, he had already lifted five dollars out of my wallet! He insisted that he had not taken it while I insisted that he had. Finally, I said that I would call the police and press charges for money he took last week unless I got it back. As I fumbled through the phone book for the number, he gave it back. I went out jogging with my wallet in one hand and my keys in the other. I thought he might destroy the house. But going out running was the best thing to do. He calmed down when I wasn't there. The rest of the evening was uneventful.

May 10, 2001

CASSP meeting for Chris at New Bloomfield, Chris and I participated along w/ Virginia Diaz, Vincent Unger, Teresa Wilson, Wanda Newman (Office of Vocational

Rehabilitation), George Peterson (Susquenita), and Barbara Sullivan of Holy Spirit. The plan is for Chris to go to Assisted Living in Carlisle.

May 16, 2001

Chris said that he had made his own Doctor's appointment today and walked to it. The physician found that his blood pressure was high. Chris also said he began bleeding from the nose while there. Just before midnight the phone rang. Chris picked up the call at the same time that I did and did not know that I was on the line. He told Young he was arranging for a kid from Wordsworth to bring down weed on Friday the 18th and did Young want any. He recounted his Dr.'s story and implied his condition was drug related.

May 17, 2001

Chris was very angry when I got home. I was unsure about what. He broke the storm window in the door, and he said not to hassle him. Evidently, school did not go well. He went to bed at 4:30 PM, woke up briefly about 1:30 AM, and finally got up when I awoke him with a phone call at 7:30 AM on 5/18 (I was already at school).

May 18, 2001

After I woke Chris (he said he wasn't going to go to school), he called to say that he had missed the van. I picked him up with the understanding that he owed me a chore. He was surly and disrespectful to me on the way down to school. I told him not to talk to me that way. He replied, "What are you going to do about it? I'll hit you right here in the car." When we got to school, I told the secretary to call the police if there were any problems. When I got home from school at about 3 PM, Chris was on the phone. I told him that it would be his phone call for the day. He disagreed. About five minutes later, I was upstairs changing when I heard him calling from an extension. I got on another extension and told him to get off the phone. He refused. The person he was calling was not home. He came upstairs and started screaming that I didn't know anything. Then, he attempted to explain his drug phone conversation of the other night. He was very disrespectful. He went downstairs and continued screaming his disrespectful diatribe. I went downstairs and grabbed the front of his shirt. I said that he would not speak that way to me. He pushed me with his arms on my shoulders. I wrapped my legs around his stomach. He carried me over to the sofa, and we plopped down on the sofa. He banged my head against the wall. Then, he bit me just above the right nipple. He banged my head against the wall again, and he again bit me although this one did not break the skin. Somewhere in all of this, he bent my fingers back and said that he would break them. I wrestled my way to the top and took him to the rug. We agreed to break it off.

End of Journal

I did not know it at the time, but Chris would never return home to live.

In And Out Of Prison

After he was incarcerated I took Chris's medication to the prison. In the next few days, I talked to him on the phone and visited with him at the prison. He was not unhappy. One of his friends was incarcerated, and he shared mutual acquaintances with some of the other inmates. Much to my surprise he asked me to bring him a photo of myself. He told my mother by phone if he returned to live with me that he would probably kill me.

Journal

May 23, 2001

There was a bail hearing today for Chris. Although I arrived a few minutes early, they had already started. It seemed as if they were trying to find some way to get him out on his own recognizance. Going home with me was easily ruled out. They were seeking a relative locally that would take him, but there were none. Chris brought up his grandfather's trust fund to go to college. I said I would not release that money for the purpose of finding him a room. Chris had to return to prison for a lack of any place else to go. I tried to bring up his mental health record and his past police record, but they said it was inappropriate for this hearing. Chris was shaking, and he ascribed this to nicotine withdraw. He said that he tells friends that he will die one of three ways: smoking, drinking, or by a bullet.

Also on May 23, I received a letter from Wordsworth, Chris's special school placement. He received 29 detention slips since March 2001. Twelve were in May. The majority of the detentions were for the disruption of class, disrespect to staff, profanity, and arguing/fighting with other students. The school was faxing his work to the prison, but Chris was refusing to do it.

June 5, 2001

I met with Mrs. Ortiz, the prison counselor. She agrees with me that the best place for Chris may be a mental health facility. She believes that Chris wants to get out of prison to party. Chris called. He said that Young, his friend, and Wendy, Chris's girlfriend, were going together. Ominously he said they would be the first people he would visit when he was released. Chris got mad. He said that they were ready to cut him loose at the bail hearing on May 23 until I showed up. He also said that his attorney said he could claim self-defense. When he called me a dick, I hung up.

June 6, 2001

Chris's final report card arrived today. He passed everything except Physical Education. I found this amazing considering he wasn't there the last three weeks and did little when he was there. Because of the failure in Phys Ed, Chris did not graduate.

Note: it is a state requirement in Pennsylvania that students must pass Phys Ed to graduate. However, exceptions can be made for special education students who have an Individual Education Plan (IEP). At some time during the spring of 2001, Chris asked me if we could use his IEP so he could graduate without passing Phys Ed. I told him there would be no exception made since the only reason he was failing Phys Ed was his lack of participation.

June 15, 2001

I talked to Mrs. Ortiz, the prison counselor. Chris plead guilty. The next hearing will be in August. Apparently the court does not meet in July. He is in solitary confinement, or "the fucking hole" as Chris calls it, for not taking his medication and for having matches in his cell. He will have to pay for his own medication. In a letter I recently received, he had apologized to me. On this day I wrote back and said actions would be needed as well as words for me to truly believe him. I included a money order for $10 so he could buy stuff at the prison canteen. I told him about new accommodations for his pet mouse, Snowball.

July 2, 2001

Visit with Chris at prison and took Nellie Neal along (past, present, or future romantic interest of Chris, it is hard to keep track). Chris says he's going to smoke a lot of dope on the day he gets out of prison. "Somebody will probably call my P.O. and I'll go back in," he said. At the meeting with the psychiatrist on June 29, he asked to be prescribed Trazodone during the day as well as at bedtime. He said it kept him calmed down (perhaps he meant tired as it originally was given to help him sleep when he was taking the Prozac). He may be depressed. He said he wouldn't mind staying in prison, and if he got out, he wouldn't bother with other people.

July 16, 2001

Larry Scott and I went to visit Chris tonight at the prison. Chris was quite hostile. He said he wanted bail in ten days, and if this did not happen, there would be problems. He refused to specify the problems. He also said that when he is released from prison "you'll see." Referring to our altercation on May 18, he said he would have killed me if I had not let him up. Still talking a lot about self-defense and putting me in prison.

<u>End of Journal</u>

In the fall of 2001, Mrs. Ortiz arranged for a Physical Education teacher from the West Perry school district, the district in which the prison is located, to instruct Chris in Phys Ed at the prison. During this time period, Chris was once again in solitary confinement. He wrote to Nellie Neal about his desire to get out of prison and take drugs.

Journal

December 16, 2001

Visit with Chris at the prison. He wanted to take $1000 out of his grandfather's fund to bail a friend out of jail. When I said no, he threatened to get me when he got out, gave me the finger, and told me to go to hell. He said he didn't want to belong to our family anymore. When I asked if that meant that he didn't want grandpa's money, he said he was entitled to it!

December 25, 2001

The holiday season was not good for Chris. He spent Christmas day in solitary confinement. He was back in the hole in early January.

January 18, 2002

Chris said he talked to his probation officer today. He told him that he does not want to go to a program. Instead, he'll serve out his sentence in prison. I'm supposed to be getting something about his fines. Also, he said to send him $300. He figures that amount should cover him for a year. No more visits or phone calls. He concluded by saying "See you in a year."

January 19, 2002

Chris called at 10 AM. When I said that it was a short year, he said he decided that phone calls were OK. But the rest still went.

<u>End of Journal</u>

In January 2002, Chris completed the Phys Ed course in prison and earned his diploma from Susquenita. Although he did not finish the course until 2002, the diploma stated that he graduated in 2001. He and I have Mrs. Ortiz to thank for this. She went out of her way to make it happen. Of all the people I dealt with over the years in regard to Chris and his problems, she was one of the best.

Throughout his incarceration at Perry County prison, I was insistent that Chris go to a mental health facility when he was released. Finally, in April of 2002, Chris left the prison to reside at New Visions Group Home, a treatment program in Shippensburg.

When I took Chris to live in the group home in Shippensburg, I hoped that the starkness in the change of living environment might have an effect on him. Shippensburg is a college town.

As we drove into town, we saw a pretty coed rollerblading down the street. Chris yelled out "Wow!" And I said, "Yeah, you don't see people like her in prison." One of the first nights he was in town he went to a "Battle of the Bands" on campus.

Chris was to receive mental health therapy at Holy Spirit Hospital while in the group home. They did another evaluation of him on May 15. The results were essentially the same as the one they completed the year before. However, this time he was also found to have an impulse control disorder as well as being an abuser of alcohol and cannabis. His Global Assessment of Functioning (GAF) score was once again 45-50. The report concluded that Chris was refusing medication.

At first Chris attended Holy Spirit for group therapy on a regular basis. But as the months went by, he failed to attend.

At the group home it become apparent that Chris was reverting to his previous self. He was using alcohol, which was against the group home's rules. There was a scene in which another member of the home accused him of dealing crack. The police were involved. Although the accusation appeared to have some substance, nothing came of it. He had a job at a bar/restaurant called the Gingerbreadman, but he reported to work sporadically.

On August 18, 2002, Chris was discharged from the group home in Shippensburg. A summary of their report:

> Mr. Rubisch has repeatedly disregarded CRR policies and procedures and general house rules. He has consumed alcohol on no less than two occasions He has ignored his curfew on numerous occasions as well as ignored day program policies. He lied about his whereabouts during planned tutoring at the Carlisle Learning Center/OIC. He brought a pet rabbit into the house without authorization. He has been verbally abusive to staff and has, on several occasions, been unnecessarily loud so that the entire house was disturbed. Mr. Rubisch has refused to work on any goals, stating that his personal life is of more importance right now.

They concluded by stating that Chris needed ongoing psychiatric treatment via medication, counseling and drug and alcohol counseling.

When Chris left the group home, I helped him find an apartment in Shippensburg. The rent would be paid from his trust fund. Everything else, utilities, food, etc., would have to be paid by himself. I hoped that this would force him to hold a job. However, he found a girlfriend, Mary, who moved in with him. Since she was employed, Chris did not have to work. He held jobs intermittently for the next six months. He got fired from the Gingerbreadman for calling off too many times. His attendance for his MH counseling at Holy Spirit was also intermittent even though on some occasions they would send a van to pick him up.

What he was doing was dealing drugs. I learned this some years later. He went to Baltimore on one occasion for drugs, and something went extremely wrong. It was so bad that to this day, he will not tell me what happened.

Mary got Chris involved in country line dancing, and I hoped he might develop a passion for it that would turn him around. Also, during 2002-03, Chris said he passed the ASVAB test to go in the Navy. I found this hard to believe. Whether it happened or not soon became irrelevant.

There were squabbles with Mary that turned violent. On more than one occasion, the landlord called me about damages Chris had caused to the apartment. The money for repairs came from his trust fund. Mary had a Protection From Abuse filed on Chris although they still lived with each other.

On Valentine's Day 2003, Mary had Chris arrested for assault. He was in prison for a brief time before being released to await the hearing. Mary left him for good. We went to the apartment, and I found it in shambles. I received a bill from the landlord for $800 for two doors that Chris destroyed while in a rage. Chris wanted me to bring him money for food, but wary that it might go to drugs, I cleaned out my cupboards of canned goods and brought them to the apartment.

The landlord offered to terminate the lease early as he had others who could move in May 1. We jumped at the opportunity. On Easter Sunday, we cleaned out the apartment for good. In doing so, I came upon Chris's W-2 forms. He grossed $199 for the entire year of 2002!

While waiting for a final hearing on the assault of Mary, I arranged for him to live in Carlisle in an old hotel, the Molly Pitcher. Carlisle was chosen as there was potential employment at many fast food places within walking distance of the hotel. Although he never got a license, Chris could drive. Getting a license involved planning: finding out when the Bureau of Motor Vehicles was open, finding a friend with a car, etc. One hallmark of Chris's life was (and still is) living in the present.

The Molly Pitcher was run down. I hoped that he would want to work to escape the conditions. To give him further incentive, I told him that I was going to initially pay the entire rent from his trust fund. However, I would be cutting it down in 10 percent increments. I would pay for nothing else. I would not even pay for food.

My plan failed. Chris found a church that had a soup kitchen. As far as the diminishing rate for the rent, it never went into effect. Before we got to the 90% rate, Chris was rearrested and incarcerated in Cumberland County Prison for disorderly conduct. In July of 2003, he was found guilty of the assault of Mary as well as the possession of drug paraphernalia. He was found guilty of the disorderly conduct charge in September.

In the fall of 2003, he was released from prison and was back in Carlisle living in a bizarre family situation. There were three generations of a family and their friends living in the home. The nominal head of the household was an elderly gentleman who seemed to be only dimly aware of the on-goings in the house. There was a baby or two and a plethora of young adults. Drug use was a foregone conclusion.

In November of 2003 Chris was arrested for simple assault and returned to prison. From there Chris made a brief appearance at a drug treatment program in Harrisburg in February 2004 before landing back in Cumberland County Prison in March 2004 for violating his parole.

Chris, at the age of twenty-two, was released from prison in January 2005. I picked him up. He was to meet a guy in front of the Giant grocery store for some unknown reason. Perhaps the guy spotted me in my coat and tie and thought I was a narc. Whatever the case he did not show. An indication of possible ecstasy usage, Chris bought three teething rings at Giant. Without asking Chris switched the station on the car radio and was blasting rap music. I suggested that we compromise and shut it off. He did so without a word.

Chris went to live in a small house in Mt. Holly. It was nice. Once again his dwindling trust fund was paying for the rent. (Note- At one point Chris's total in the trust fund was over $12,000. Eventually, the entire amount was exhausted on rent, fines, and damages.) He had a job in Carlisle at a Wendy's. Mt. Holly to Carlisle is about six miles. His transportation to work was a ride from his girlfriend's mother. He was not living with his girlfriend. I told him I saw this as a problem. Inevitably the two of them would be scheduled for different shifts, or they would breakup. I suggested a bicycle, but he was against it. I suggested applying for a job at a convenience store that was around the corner from his home. He could tell the store manager of his proximity and say he could be available on short notice to work. Chris would have none of it.

Perhaps inevitably Chris ended up back in Cumberland County prison. He had a beer party, and there was plenty of evidence with the empty cans engulfing the outdoor garbage can. Drinking was against his probation. Tipped off by his spiteful girlfriend, his probation officer arrested him in April 2005.

Chris remained in Cumberland County Prison from the spring of 2005 until November of the same year. Prior to his release Chris talked of going to live with friends in Texas or North Carolina. He said he would be fine if he could get out of the state of Pennsylvania. Ultimately he decided upon going to New Hampshire to stay with a young woman, her infant, and the young woman's mother. He met this woman via the internet while he was living in Shippensburg and had stayed in touch with her over the years.

I thought his choice was questionable. He talked of going to NH to protect "Mom" (as he already referred to the older woman of the two) from her new husband (apparently a live in boyfriend). Allegedly he beat her up while he was drunk. I called the older woman to warn her about Chris, but she did not revoke her offer.

New Hampshire

On November 15, 2005, I picked up twenty-three old Chris and took him to Baltimore-Washington International Airport for his flight to New Hampshire. Chris was released even though there was a major altercation in the prison the previous day. Apparently Chris owed another inmate money. The other man, knowing that Chris was about to be released, stole Chris's sneakers as repayment. Chris went after him with a metal mop ringer. He was released anyway. Cumberland County must have been glad to get rid of him.

Chris's stay with his new family did not go bad immediately. The older woman found him a job working at a printing facility. Chris discovered the younger woman was not interested in him romantically and seemed to be able to accept this. But before too long, he reverted to his old habits of drug and alcohol usage. The older woman tried to keep him at home in the evening, but he was not interested. There were problems at work as well. Perhaps inevitably, Chris was out of the home and out of a job.

As the year 2006 began, Chris moved from home to home and girlfriend to girlfriend. Beside his girlfriend of the moment, there were numerous dalliances on the side. His choice of drug was anything he could get his hands on. One girlfriend remembers the first time she met him, he was scratching and dry heaving to the point she did not think that he would survive.

On February 16, 2006 Chris was transported by the Somersworth Police to the emergency room of Community Partners in Strafford County, New Hampshire. He listed an address in Somersworth as his home. It was not the home of the family he had initially lived with in New Hampshire.

Chris told the police he had been partying with some friends and his girlfriend of one month. They were using alcohol and marijuana. He became upset about a conversation and arguing ensued. He asked to be left alone. When that did not occur, he walked out of the house to the police station. He told the police he would hurt himself or others if he had stayed. He reported losing his job a week before.

Two months later on the evening of April 10, 2006, an ambulance was summoned to the Somersworth Police Department. Chris was at the police station with a lacerated left wrist. He said he was walking down the street and had been assaulted by a knife-wielding assailant. Later he was to say that this was a suicide attempt due to an argument with his girlfriend.

The following is Chris's own account of his life during this time period. It is apparently a letter to a person unknown. It should be noted that Chris his prone to bravado and fabrication.

> Around June 2006, I was living at Hampton Beach on "N" street. During the week that I was there (Hampton Beach). And on the weekends, I could be found on the corner of South and Green Streets in Somersworth, partying. And I continued this throughout the summer. Besides the partying I was in Somersworth to re-up my stash and to drop off my cash made, that week before. I was

working for a guy that I know called "Q". I was selling…weed, and shrooms for "Q" that summer. Things were going fine until I started snorting oxy cottons (sic). It was then that "Q" noticed that his money was becoming lighter then what it was supposed to be. One weekend when he came to pick me up in his red Chrysler…He asked me about the shortage of money. I told him that I was sorry and that I would find a way to pay the money back. So then me and two friends decided that at some point we were going to break into some cars and houses and pull a "smash and grab." We got caught and got locked up in Rockingham County Prison. I went back to Somersworth where I met up with a girl by the name of Patty. Her and I had a quick but subtle sexual relationship with one another. Which didn't last long. Due to the two of us getting caught by one of "Q's" boys…When her and I tried to break into his place to rob him. That was my decision to rob him. And we were only there to steal his stash and cash. After that "Q" made 2 attempts to get even. When he finally became successful in getting even with me. The first two attempts were made at "Burby's", well, outside of Burby's. First "Q" tried to drag me to his car. Then later that same night, he tried to stab me with an unknown object. Both times my boy Billy stopped him. A couple of days went by. Then one night me and my boy Mike from Franklin St., were walking towards "Burby's" in search for Patty. When she was not found, we left and headed back to his place. We were walking up a street (whose name I can' remember) when we were flagged down by "Q's" car. Only he wasn't driving. There were three people in the car…Gladys who was drinking and some other girl in the front passenger, and Maria in the back seat. Me and Mike smoked a joint with them until two cops rolled up on us from both sides of the car. Mike was arrested for possession. And I too was charged. Even though the weed belonged to the girl in the passenger (seat). When Mike's wife came, the police left us go. We walked to his house, but left shortly after that. We were headed to Maria's house. There was a party going on outside Q's house. That's when he snuffed me and beat the shit out of me for breaking into his house. That and I owed him $50. Which I never paid.

Chris was charged with receiving stolen property in June of 2006 and was incarcerated in Strafford County Prison. During the first six months of 2006, he was also arrested for filing a false report re: the phony assault in April, and once in Maine for possession of marijuana and paraphernalia. He was released from prison at the end of July. He went to the home of Margaret Ibarra as she always let him store his possessions at her home. It was there that he met Diane Bell.

Diane and her infant son, Mateusz (commonly known as Matty), had also been transient. Incredibly Chris and Diane knew each other from the time he had lived in Carlisle, Pa. in 2003. In July 2006 Diane was living with Holly Kelly and her two children. Chris moved in with them.

On August 23, 2006 Chris was involved in a confrontation with a relative of Diane in Berwick, Maine, which is just across the Salmon Falls River from Somersworth, NH. Chris and the relative became argumentative, and the latter asked Chris to leave the home (which belonged to her father). Chris was holding Diane's baby, Matty. He claimed the relative was pointing her finger in his face and actually jabbed him with it. According to Chris, he responded, "Look, I'm telling you right now if you don't get your fucking finger out of my fucking face, I'm going to punch you in your fucking mouth. You fuck with me, bitch, I dare you."

At this point, Chris said he placed Matty on a sofa. Diane confirms his account. However, the relative and another eyewitness, Margaret Ibarra, said Chris threw Matty to the sofa. The confrontation became physical with some accounts saying the relative threw the first punch. Others said Christopher did. Chris acknowledges hitting her twice in the face and once alongside of the head. Her father became involved and stopped the fight. According to the relative, Chris threatened to kill her if she went to the police.

Three days later she did go to the police. Her injuries were still visible on that day.

Also on August 26, 2008 the Somersworth Police interviewed Irene Phillips. While she was walking down the street, a male and a female confronted her. She knew only the female, Diane. Diane grabbed Irene by the arm and told her she and her boyfriend, CJ (Chris often went by his initials), had beaten up a woman who lives in Maine (in a reference to Diane's relative). Diane said CJ had thrown her son on a couch. At the completion of this story, Chris and Diane told Irene they would retaliate and harm her if she told anyone. (Note: Chris claims the confrontation with Irene Phillips never occurred.)

According to Diane she and Chris argued the evening of the

The Incident

August 27, 2006

Chris and Diane slept on the floor that night. Matty awoke about 5:30 AM, and Chris fed him. He then returned to sleep. Matty and Diane awoke about 9 :00 AM. Chris arose between 10:30 and 11:00 AM. Diane's father arrived at 1:15 PM to take his daughter to Walmart. Chris was told by Diane to watch Matty and to feed him a bottle.

Diane was gone for a short time. Accounts vary as to how long. When she returned home, a neighbor, Theresa Hughes, said there had been an accident. Hughes said she became aware something was wrong when she heard Chris calling for her roommate, Susan Ybarra. Ybarra and Chris brought Matty to the porch and placed him on a large wooden cable spool, which served as a table. Hughes noted Matty's pupils appeared to be dilated, and he was not responsive to light. She also noted the baby was having difficulty breathing as he was gasping for breath. Matty was not crying, whimpering, or making any sound. Hughes described the baby's appearance as that of a rag doll. She saw no blood or bruises on the baby when he was handed to her. Chris told her that the baby fell down the stairs. He was frantic. Hughes called 911.

The Somersworth Police Department received the call at about 1:50 while at a softball game with the fire department (it was a Sunday). Patrolman Nicholas Skiba was the first responding officer from the SPD to arrive on the scene. When he arrived at the residence, Officer Skiba observed three adults standing over a small wooden table on a porch adjacent to 17 West Green Street. The adults were Diane Bell, Theresa Hughes, and Chris Rubisch. Officer Skiba noted that there was an infant lying on the table. He approached the child and noticed the child had a faint heartbeat and appeared to be having difficulty breathing. When medical personnel arrived, Officer Skiba spoke to Diane. Diane stated that the baby had fallen down the stairs, but she was not home when it occurred. She stated that "C.J." had been watching the baby while she was out. When Officer Skiba asked who that was, Diane pointed to a man that Officer Skiba recognized from prior contacts as being Christopher Rubisch.

Chris offered Officer Skiba an explanation as to what had happened. After Diane left with her father, he went upstairs to retrieve some items. He was carrying Matty at the time and put him down at the top of the stairs to enter the bedroom. As Chris returned to go back down the stairs, Matty fell down the stairs face forward. There were approximately eleven stairs. Chris went down the stairs to pick up the child and held him. Matty was crying at first but eventually calmed down. Chris took Matty into the living room where he sat him on the couch to watch television. Within 5-10 minutes, Chris noticed that Matty seemed to be slumped over and inactive. Chris said he picked Matty up and noticed that he was not breathing normally. Consequently, he ran over to the neighbors and called 911. Officer Skiba asked why Chris had not called 911 from the phone in his half of the duplex. Chris began to yell at the officer that he thought there was something he might have been able to do himself to help the child, and he did not have a book on this stuff.

Matty was taken to Wentworth-Douglas Hospital in Dover, New Hampshire. Chris agreed to go to the police station to discuss the situation further. When Chris got to the station, he met with a Detective John Kelly. At first Chris stuck with his story of Matty falling down the stairs. During a break in the interview process, Detective Kelly talked to a doctor at Wentworth Douglas Hospital. The doctor informed Detective Kelly that the baby's injuries were the result of abuse and not an accident. Matty had three separate subdural hematomas: on his collarbone, his backside, and from his mid-back to mid-thigh. He also had bi-lateral collapsed lungs. Due to the severity of the injuries, he was being transported to Boston Children's Hospital.

Detective Kelly returned to the room. He asked Chris about what had happened in

Berwick, ME., the confrontation with Diane's relative, in which he allegedly threw Matty on the sofa. Chris became irate and started yelling at Detective Kelly that nothing happened. Detective Kelly advised Chris to calm down and to stop yelling. He explained to Chris what he had learned about Matty's medical state. At that point Chris asked if he could go outside to smoke a cigarette, and Detective Kelly went with him. After lighting the cigarette, Chris said, "I fucked up." He went on to say that the baby was crying, and he could not console Matty. So he spanked him on the "ass, probably harder than I should have".

Chris stated that the baby would not stop crying, and he shook it. As Matty continued to cry, Chris shook him again and again. After finishing the cigarette Chris asked Detective Kelly if he could speak to him inside alone. He said he did not want the conversation recorded. The conversation was not recorded. However, Chris did not know the video camera in the room they used was still active, and the picture and sound were being seen and heard by police personnel in another room.

In his second revised accounting of the incident, Chris gave more details. He said he had a lot of things to do, but he was unable to do them because Matty was crying. He tried giving him a bottle and laying him down, but the baby continued to cry. He tried unsuccessfully to ignore him. Picking him up under the arm pits, Chris began to shake Matty and yelled, "What the fuck is wrong with you, what do you want me to do?" The baby's head was moving back and forth due to the shaking. He shook him a second time. Matty was unresponsive after the shaking. Chris then went to the neighbors for help.

After this account of the incident, Chris began to cry and was emotional for a long time period. He asked if he could go outside for another smoke. Initially told no, he became agitated, and the detectives allowed him to go out with two escorts. Nothing was said during this break. When Chris reentered, he was read his Miranda rights and was arrested. Chris waived his rights and again gave an account of the incident, which included the shaking and the spankings. Chris was transported to the Strafford County House of Corrections. He was charged with first-degree assault. Chris was put on suicide watch and was seen by Community Partners Emergency Services Crisis.

August 28, 2006

Chris met with Detective Kelly and Sgt Mike Nolan. He again talked about the incident. Some of the details were different, but the story was essentially the same. Chris talked about how much he loved Matty and wanted to adopt him. Matty was cutting teeth according to Chris. He also said he was frustrated from an argument with Diane the night before. The topic of the argument was not specified. Several times Chris asked for the interview to be terminated, but it was not.

On this day there was an ominous report from Children's Hospital in Boston. It was discovered there was bleeding in Matty's brain. The color of the bruises, from his lower back to his mid-thighs, was blue-purple indicating significant bleeding. A doctor of Boston Children's Hospital said the injuries to the lungs must have occurred just before the 911 call. Otherwise, Matty would not have survived. He went on to say there was a skull fracture caused by a blow to the head. Matty was put on a breathing machine and was given medication in case he had seizures.

Notes from Children and Youth on this date state, "If he (Matty) survives, they may have to talk about withdrawing life support."

August 29, 2006

The New Hampshire media was full of Chris today. I got on their websites. A neighbor was quoted as saying about Chris, ""I want him gone for life. I want him gone to prison for life." The baby is reported to have a punctured lung and brain swelling. I talked to Chris's lawyer on the phone. She said she was hoping to hear from someone like me. I told her about all the documentation I had including the MRI of Chris's brain damage. She wants the MRI sent to her. When I asked if Chris was under the influence of something during the incident, she did not comment. As it will only whip up the media, she wants to waive the hearing in early September. I talked to Chris on the phone, and he was back to his surly self. He wanted a private attorney and $250,000 for bail.

For me the day was like being on an emotional roller coaster. It was hard to see my son reduced to a caricature of a villain by the media. I was happy to have a chance to help him through the attorney. As for the possibility of bail, it was a non-starter. If released Chris in all likelihood would commit another crime.

August 31, 2006

I talked to Chris on the phone. He talked to his uncle by phone. He says that he won't be out of prison until he's 35. At that time he'll have no reason to live, and he'll commit suicide. Who will hire a 35-year old baby beater he said.

September 15, 2006

From Children and Youth notes: Matty fails swallowing test. Has a feeding tube. Talk about placing him in rehab.

September 26, 2006

Notes from prison dispensary: Chris in good spirits and denies suicide intention. Anger at self for what happened.

October 17, 2006

Matty was admitted to Cedarcrest Center for Children with disabilities. His condition at the time:

Mateusz had very significant injuries, including diffuse hypoxic ischemic brain injury: bilateral pulmonary contusions; bilateral pneumothoraces; s/p (status post) bilateral chest tubes; subdural hemorrhages; retinal hemorrhages and subarachnoid hemorrhage.

His hearing is felt to be within normal ranges. His vision is severely impaired. He quiets when picked up and shows pleasure with touch and handling. Mateusz enjoys his pacifier but has great difficult holding it in place in his mouth. Therapy is working with him to strengthen his suck and has also trialed multiple pacifiers to determine which is the best for him. He seems to be sensitive to light and a baseball cap with a large brim, as well as sunglasses, have been trialed. Mateusz has increased tone in his trunk and extremities.

October 23, 2006

Chris is twenty-four today. He punched a window in booking resulting in pain in his right hand and wrist. He cannot make a full fist.

October 30, 2006

It is discovered that Chris is writing letters to a female inmate, Karen Nunez. In the letters it states, "Your (sic) right, I'm a baby shaker. Otherwise I wouldn't be here. I fucked up, and I know it." Elsewhere in the letter, hand written in purple ink by someone else is, "Baby shawkin piece of shit. No' one cares what you got to say."

In his letter to her, Chris says that he is going to stay in his cell otherwise "somebody is gonna end up with the mop ringer permanently attached to their skull." Chris goes on to say that he wrote the woman's mother and asked for her hand in marriage.

December 12, 2006: (Almost four months after The Incident)

Notes on Matty from a Dr. at Cedarcrest: Matty no longer has seizures as was the case at the hospital. He has no respiratory problems.

February 7, 2007

According to a preliminary examination by a forensic psychologist who saw the records I mailed to New Hampshire, Chris's temporal lobe brain lesion may result in the loss of control of emotions and a labile temper.

March 7, 2007

I got a call at 4 PM call from Olivia Taylor, the assistant to Chris's attorney. Matty has died. No details. Chris could now be charged with homicide. There would be a mandatory sentence of 35 years since it was a child.

March 7, 2007 (March 8 in print)

From the *Manchester Union Leader*

SOMERSWORTH - An infant severely shaken last August died from his injuries Tuesday night, and the man accused of assaulting the baby may now face a murder charge.

Mateusz Bell was 8 months old when he was allegedly shaken with such force last summer he got brain damage and never recovered. He died at Dartmouth-Hitchcock Medical Center about 8 p.m. Tuesday after being treated at numerous hospitals over the past several months.

An autopsy performed yesterday showed Bell died of complications from blunt impact injuries to his head. His death was ruled a homicide.

Prosecutors expect to upgrade charges against 24-year-old Christopher Rubisch of Somersworth. Rubisch, the former boyfriend of Bell's mother, is currently charged with first- and second-degree assault for allegedly shaking and spanking the child.

"In all likelihood, the charges will be upgraded," Assistant Attorney General Karen Huntress said yesterday.

Rubisch is not Bell's father. His trial on the assault charges is scheduled for September.

Diane Bell, her son Mateusz, and Rubisch were staying temporarily at 17 West Green St.

last August with a friend, (name omitted). On Aug. 27 at about 2 p.m., police responded to the home after receiving a report of an unresponsive infant. They found the infant severely injured. He was first taken to Wentworth-Douglas Hospital in Dover for treatment and soon after to Children's Hospital in Boston.

Since being hurt, Bell has suffered immeasurably," (name omitted) said yesterday. It has been one medical problem after another, she said.

"Every little thing was a huge hurdle," she said.

(name omitted) said Bell's mother took him off a respirator on Monday, and he died about 18 hours later. He was 14 months old.

"It's better this way because he had been suffering," (name omitted) said. "He went to sleep and just didn't wake up." (name omitted) said Diane Bell was overcome with grief and did not want to speak to reporters yesterday.

End of *Manchester Union Leader* article

A Follow Up report:

State Says Baby's Death was a Murder

State and local law enforcement authorities reported this afternoon that a 14-month-old Somersworth infant who suffered severe brain injuries on August 27, 2006 - allegedly as a result of shaking by a man who faces criminal charges -

died yesterday at Dartmouth-Hitchcock Medical Center in Lebanon. The death has been ruled a homicide.

According to a press release from the state attorney general, emergency personnel responded to 17-19 West Green Street in Somersworth after receiving a report of an unresponsive infant. The then-8-month-old was transported to Wentworth-Douglas Hospital, then to Children's Hospital in Boston.

Christopher Rubisch, 24, was arrested and charged with first degree assault for shaking the infant and causing brain injuries, and with second degree assault for spanking the child and causing bruising.

Chief Medical Examiner Dr. Thomas A. Andrew conducted an autopsy today, and determined the cause of the child's death to be complications from blunt impact injuries to his head. The Attorney General's Office has not yet determined if charges will be upgraded.

End of Follow Up Report

In fact, these reports in the media told only half the story. Here is the conclusion straight from the autopsy report:

1. Acute opiate intoxication (free morphine 2700 ng/mL)

2. Blunt impact injury of head, remote (see accompanying Neuropathology Report).
   a. Cerebral atrophy, marked
   b. Subdural hygromas, bilateral

    c.   Bilateral retinal hemorrhages (anamnestic), residual hemosiderin pigment on histological evaluation.

3.   Axpiration (terminal) of gastric content, right lung

CONCLUSION:

It is my opinion, that Mateusz Bell, a 14-month-old white male died as a result of respiratory failure secondary to administration of morphine. The decedent had sustained severe neurological injury as a result of abuse at the age of six months. Morphine was administrated in the context of extubation after declaring the deceased "DNR" for observed discomfort after extubation. Review of the medical records shows the decedent received 34 mg of morphine sulfate intravenously, in seven different doses in the 50 minutes prior to his death. This is a dosage of 3.1 mg per kilogram per hour. Standard analgesic doses are in the range of 0.1 to 0.2 mg/kg repeated every four hours as needed. The average blood level of morphine in fatal morphine intoxication cases is approximately 700 ng/ml a level greatly exceeded in this case as noted above. Based on circumstances surrounding the death as currently known, the manner of death is homicide.

CAUSE OF DEATH:

Respiratory failure due to opiate intoxication following administration of morphine for the management of delayed sequelae of blunt impact injury of head.

MANNER OF DEATH:

Homicide.

End of Autopsy

If Diane Bell took her son off the respirator on Monday March 5, what happened in the intervening time before Matty's death? (Note that name omitted gives the time frame as 18 hours, which does not exactly match up with the 8 PM time of death on Tuesday March 6). He survived the extubation from life support. Still alive, many hours later, he was injected with a lethal dose of morphine at Dartmouth Hitchcock Medical Center. Lebanon, N.H. Thus, the conclusion of homicide. However, Chris could not have done it as he was in prison. More disturbing is that Chris and Chris's attorney told me that Diane Bell was never consulted regarding the final decision to end her son's life.

Matty's death is not being investigated.

I talked to Chris on April 2,3, and 6 of 2007. For the first time he acknowledged being on drugs at the time of the incident, Crystal Meth. He also implied that someone else might have harmed Matty. He wasn't a snitch he said. If he snitched people would be after me, his cousins, and a lot of our family. He said he would go to prison for 25 years rather than snitch. He said he had "got his ass handed to him" several times since moving to NH and implied that he was selling drugs. I talked to the assistant of the attorney during this time period re: Chris's tirade. She said Chris was on the ledge. There was a big confrontation when the baby died. The prison wanted to move him for his own safety, but he refused to do so. They had to forcibly carry him out. On the sixth he said he had written a letter to fire his attorney and was going to give it to him that day. Chris wants to take the offense and sue the state of NH for not getting him mental health help. The assistant said that they were contemplating taking that action, but they did not want to release all his info prior to trial. It occurred to me through all of this that Chris had not changed. One cannot reason with him. He wants what he wants. The issues have changed since he was young, but he is the same.

April 16, 2007

The forensic psychologist hired by Chris's legal team has concluded Chris's brain abnormality significantly contributed to his conduct at the time of his alleged offense. "Mr. Rubisch has a brain injury in his left temporal lobe that has likely been present since birth and that involves a specific area of the brain known to affect mood and aggression."

June 2007

Chris's attorney filed a motion to suppress Chris's confession as Chris had not been read his Miranda rights prior to his confession. Chris confessed to Detective Kelly while outside taking a smoke. There was no recording device present. Chris came inside and confessed without being recorded. He got a second smoke outside and then was read his Miranda rights. Subsequently, he gave the same confession. The state argued that Chris voluntarily said, "I fucked up," while outside the building taking the first smoke. Furthermore, the state argued that Miranda is to be given if the suspect is "in custody," and Chris was not in custody at the station. On Monday August 28th the detectives refused to terminate the interview even though Chris requested they do so. The state acknowledged that the interview should have been terminated on the August 28th. In regards to the interviews on the 27th and the 28th, Chris said that he knew his rights before they were given to him.

Between June of 2007 and January of 2008, the trial often seemed to be on again off again. There were times I wondered what Chris was thinking. On one occasion he requested to borrow my zoot suit (which I wear for swing dancing) to wear to the hearing.

Rather suddenly the hearing was held on January 28, 2008. Chris pled guilty to 1st and 2nd degree assault. Chris was sentenced to two consecutive 10-20 year terms. Quote from the judge, "It's a long sentence, but I think it's rightfully deserved. You've taken away a life."

Chris will serve twenty to thirty years. At a minimum he could be out in 2026. He would be forty-four years old.

I have mixed feelings about the sentence. I thought it was excessive for an assault charge. However, at the same time, although he did not actually kill Matty Bell, he did take away from him the chance of leading a productive life. I was relieved that others and myself would no longer be threatened by his presence in society. I thought others would be safe from Chris, and Chris would be safe from others. While he was in prison.

I was wrong on both counts.

Incarcerated

Since he was sentenced Chris has bounced back and forth between the correctional facilities at Concord and Berlin due to his behavior. Even incarcerated he has difficulty in controlling himself. He has spent more than one Christmas day in solitary confinement. One would think this would result in self-examination, but apparently in his case, it does not.

August 21, 2008

Letter from Chris. He wants to take a correspondence course through Louisiana State University. I arrange this, but he does not follow through in completion of the course.

August 3, 2010

I received a call from Dr. Thomas, Northern Correctional facility, Berlin, NH. An MRI discovered a precise lesion. Chris has temporal lobe epilepsy (TLE). More tests will be done including a full neurology workup. He is recommending a second MRI. Chris has a benign tumor in the brain. The TLE may result in Chris perseverating in a behavior. The left hippocampus, central core, and the left temporal lobe, are smaller in volume than is normal.

January 26, 2012

Letter from Chris. He has a job in the prison.

July 31, 2013

I meet with Chris at the prison for a visit. If the incident had not happened with Matty, he said he probably would have died from drug usage before the year was over. In the first half of 2006, he said he almost drowned in a bathtub while he was high.

October 18, 2013

Chris is jumped and seriously beaten in prison. As the assault occurred in the dark, his assailants are unknown. He says he knows of no one that had a motive (I found out later that this was not true). The left half of his face was beaten to the point that it might need reconstructive surgery. His left eye was swollen nearly shut.

November 17, 2013

Received a call from Chris today. He had been in solitary confinement. Now he is back in the medical facilities of the prison. They have done some reconstructive surgery to his face. His face hurts. He has migraines. His face is numb. His nose is fine. He said something about the bottom half of his eyeball, which was unclear. He told the prison administration who inflicted the injuries. Apparently it was a prison gang trying to extort money from him.

The prison administration told him they could put him in protective custody, but this would not guarantee his safety. If he was in protective custody, Chris said he would be unable to receive things shipped to him from outside the prison. He sent a letter to the New Hampshire Civil Liberties Union through his girlfriend in regards to what he believes is negligence on part of the prison in regards to the beating. Not trusting the prison officials, he sent the letter to the NHCLU within his letter to her. If the perpetrator pays restitution, it goes to the prison for the cost of the medical services.

November 23, 2013

Call from Chris. He says Captain Owens at Berlin blocks him from returning to Berlin supposedly because he threatened staff at that facility. He has yet to receive mail from NHCLU.

December 26, 2013

Chris returns to Berlin. NHCLU and a private attorney are not interested in helping Chris take legal action against the prison for having been beat up.

March 1, 2014

I visit Chris at Concord. It did not take much to get him upset. He became very agitated by just talking about a past confrontation that he thought was unjust. He has two plates and four screws in his face.

There was a slight bump on his right cheek, which was barely perceptible. One might think it was swollen. He said his right eye was lower than the left, but I did not notice it until he pointed it out. He has requested to be placed in a prison in another state. There was a problem at Berlin, and he is now back in Concord. While at Berlin he became agitated because he could not see his counselor. Later on that day he was called down and walked into a room with three women, one his counselor. According to Chris whenever he was in a room with these three individuals in the past the results were always bad. So he walked out. This was enough reason to ship him back to Concord. He has been at Concord five times and Berlin four times. He has contacted two journalists regarding his beatings. He said the beating occurred because of the crime he committed. He says he can sleep up to sixteen hours a day! He said the only medication he is on is Seroquel. While I was there a guard abruptly tried to end the three-hour visit early. I'd guess we were 45 minutes into the visit (I did not have my watch as the prison would not let me bring it in). The guard said they needed the room. I stayed until the end after Chris protested vociferously. Again, when it was time to leave, he protested asking for another hour. When he was agitated during the visit, he got so loud I thought they might terminate the visit. He said one judge in Strafford County said he needed mental health placement instead of prison as he would get worse if incarcerated. He said that was exactly what has happened.

July 2, 2014

I visited Chris at Concord. It did not go well. Near the end of the visit, he told me he wanted me to put money on his phone so he can call people. He has had his phone privileges suspended, but he had found a work around as he had another inmate's personal code number. When I told him that I am not going to do this, he lost it and yelled, "It is a good thing there is this glass window between you and me." I walked out of the visit early.

Conclusion

Looking back on it now, I know there were good times with Chris. One was going to Dorney (Amusement) Park in Allentown when he was young. Another, when he was a little older, was when we went to see an exhibition of military drill teams and marching bands at the Capital Center in Maryland. A third was attending a Penn State-Purdue football game when he was an adolescent. But those times were overshadowed by the fact that I was always on edge knowing he could explode at any time. Every night before I went to sleep, I would count to 300 to assure myself he was indeed asleep and would not get up and do something. After he started the fire in 1993, I placed a fire extinguisher next to my bed. Some nights I knew the next day was going to be pure hell. I was never wrong. Occasionally I would pray one of us would die rather than to have to face that next day.

Some people, who knew of our problems, would say that I was a hero. I never felt like one. I just did what had to be done. Others would say "God gave him to you because he knew you could handle him." I hated that one. What it really meant was thank God I don't have him.

Now and then there are reminders of the bad old days. My wedding ring is gone. Chris admitted he traded it for drugs. Within the last three years, I searched for my buffalo nickel collection that my father and I had worked on when I was young. With his death in 2011, it meant more to me. Or would have meant more to me. It was gone for drugs as well.

I hear from Chris periodically mostly when he wants money or to get information from the internet. I see him twice a year usually at Christmas and during the summer. I am the only visitor he gets other than a sporadic girlfriend. Yes, amazingly, he still has women interested in him. Some people feel I should see him more regularly. Others wonder why I bother with him at all. Twice a year just seems right to me.

Occasionally during visits he'll say something that will give me hope that he may really change. It is amazing I can still get that spark every once in a while. However, my rational side knows better. Similarly, I used to blame myself for what happened. I still get that feeling now and then, but its frequency has diminished over the years.

My life with Christopher was one of diminishing expectations: he'll go to college! He'll enlist in the military! He can go to Vo-Tech! Maybe we can get him through high school. Maybe he can stay out of prison. He won't stay out of prison. Something bad is going to happen. Something bad did happen.

When he was young my worst fear was that I would raise a child that would end up incarcerated. That fear came true and even more so. As a friend once said, the only people more reviled than Chris are those that ran the planes into the World Trade Center.

Now that my worst fear has come true, what do I do? I live with it.

And I write a book about it so in the future some parents and their children may know the one thing I would do differently if I had to do it over again: don't place too much trust or reliance on the American mental health system.

That's the least I can do for Matty Bell.

Missed Opportunities

Mateusz "Matty" Bell did not have to die. The circle of physical abuse that began when Christopher had his clavicle broken in 1983 and was completed in 2006 with his shaking of Matty could have been stopped many times.

The first was when Chris was not yet two years old and was seen by Albert Einstein Medical Center in Philadelphia. Their evaluation on October 19, 1984:

> Referred because worried about temper tantrums. Head banging two to three times a day. Will eat excessively until he throws up. At birth, head circumference of 31.5 cm was small for length of body 48.26 cm (19 in). Climb stairs at 21 months. (Note- this is a developmental lag).
>
> Very frightened and reserved during exam. Height at 30th percentile, weight at 25, head circumference was 45.2 cm, less than 5th percentile. Demonstrated head titubation- swaying of head, on an intermittent basis. Impression- Familial developmental delay with secondary social and emotional deprivation.

The conclusion is that his genes and his environment were responsible for the way he was. One could have given that summary before the appointment. Temper tantrums, head banging, head titubation, a small head size yet no one thought to do a CAT scan? And how about the word impression? The Children and Youth agency did not send him all the way to Philadelphia to get an "impression." Why was there not a more definitive statement? Because they did not spend significant time with him to make one? Perhaps that was because at that time, before he was adopted, Chris was a poor kid on welfare.

That CAT scan was eventually done fourteen years later in 1997, and it was not until that point in Chris's life that the brain damage was discovered. If that information had been available earlier, the misdiagnosis of ADHD might have been avoided.

I question how much the medical community knew about ADHD in the eighties. I remember going to a parental support group. The professional speaking talked as if ADHD had been cured: give kids the medication and just monitor them for negative side effects. I raised my hand and said I thought I could handle the hyperactivity, but it was the defiance I found troublesome. The professional responded he thought oppositional behavior occurred in only a minority of cases. This provoked an immediate response from many in the audience that they had difficulties with defiance as well.

Chris and I got on the great ADHD assembly line of the late eighties and early nineties: give kids meds for hyperactivity, if they don't quite fit the ADHD diagnosis, make them fit. If the meds don't work, try another kind. Holy Spirit and Transact both did this even though the psychiatrist at the latter appeared to have an inkling that there was something more serious going on with Chris. It took moving to State College and meeting with a general practitioner to look outside the ADHD box.

There were plenty of indications earlier that Chris's brain was damaged. From the drawings he did for the psychiatrist in 1989, to the Bender-Gestalt given a year later, to the Bender given in 1992, Chris's drawings gave indications of organicity, brain damage. I read these findings and did not realize the extent of his damage until the MRI in 1997. Other people read the results as well. But treatment did not change. We continued on the ADHD assembly line.

I did not realize the significance of the mentioned brain damage because I made the false assumption the mental health community was looking out for what was best for my son. Let's again look at his discharge summary from The Meadows in 1997:

> The results of the current evaluation are not indicative of a psychotic, manic, or neuropsychological impairment contributing to his socially disruptive and self-destructive behaviors.

This is disingenuous at best. The key word in the previous paragraph is current. Perhaps The Meadows's evaluation did not show signs of neurological impairment, but at least three and arguably a fourth had done so previously.

Discharge statements in mental health are written to rationalize the organizations' actions. As mentioned earlier Dr. Xiong wrote a glowing discharge statement of how well Chris was doing in 1992 despite multiple reports otherwise. His concluding statement was "Chris was lost to medication clinic subsequent to the November 11, 1992 session." It sounds as if he fell off a boat in the Atlantic. But it sounded better than saying that Mr. Rubisch was totally dissatisfied with the treatment his son received through Holy Spirit.

Another case is the discharge statement by The Meadows Outpatient Psychiatric Program in Harrisburg in March of 1996-"By March 4, 1998, it was the decision of the entire

Treatment Team that this patient's behavior was creating a risky situation to himself and to his father."

The hell it was. I had to pull strings to get him in the program. As my friend David Yates said, they weren't going to take him at inpatient for the second time because they had already exhausted my insurance money and would have got paid at a lower rate by welfare.

Money. Decisions were frequently made in the MH system based on money. I believe that Chris was sent home by The Meadows in December of 1997, despite being labeled as having ODD and Borderline personality traits (both of which are extremely difficult to treat), because his insurance payments were exhausted or nearly exhausted.

Money. His second time around in The Meadows, during the Spring of 1997, I asked if I could take Chris to see his ice hockey team (he played for them while not hospitalized) in their championship game. Dr. King said no. I found this hard to believe. I pointed out that Chris would be "contained" during this excursion. There would be a two-hour ride in the car to Hershey, we would watch the game at a nearly empty Hershey Arena, and then return two hours in the car. Dr. King said that what I said made sense, but "they" (undefined as to who they were but one can assume he meant the insurance providers) would take this as proof that Chris did not need to be hospitalized despite all indications otherwise. It should also be noted that The Meadows would not be reimbursed for the time Chris was at the hockey game.

Money. On one occasion we went to see a psychiatrist in Lancaster. This was our first appointment with him. I was determined we would get somewhere this time. I brought all of Chris's records with me. I figured if someone would just take the time to examine all the tests results, anecdotal evidence, etc., we would find a solution. Our appointment was at 1:50 PM.

Christopher's Story:
An Indictment Of The American Mental Health System

The time should have tipped me off. When I started going through the stack of material, a look of panic came across the face of the psychiatrist. I said something about changing his medication, and I had done some research on my own on lithium. His response was a hurried, yes, lithium, and he started to write a script. When I voiced my frustration that he was not listening, he said that he was to give each patient only ten minutes before moving on to the next! Ten minutes: enough time to ask if the current medication worked, and if it had any side effects but no time to solve problems.

Money. Last but certainly not least, there was the discharge from the day treatment program when he needed to attend the last day for closure until there was a snowstorm. Snow may cancel school, but apparently it did not cancel billable hours.

It is difficult to determine how much money played a role in the last chance to avert Chris from the destructive path he was to follow in life. It may have been just gross incompetence in the early months of 2001, which kept the mental health system from doing what needed to be done: place him in an institution. On January 31, 2001, Ian Ingram refused to consider placement for Chris even though both Chris and I were requesting it. Ingram knew Chris from the days we saw him for counseling. He knew when Chris was of elementary school age he had once killed a pet rat in a fit of rage. Cruelty to animals by children is a red flag. Yet, not only did Ingram refuse to consider placement, he misdirected our pleas for help by sending us to an unneeded drug and alcohol evaluation. His notes from that day said to file our case until further contact. We were asking every day for help and not getting it from MH.

The MH system was (and still is) overburdened with cases. It took us two months to get an appointment with a psychiatrist. The one caseworker had over 700 cases on her

The Mental Health System

I know that one of the criticisms of this book may be that I am writing about events that happened, in some cases, two decades ago. One might think that the mental health system has surely improved in the intervening years.

From my vantage point as a high school counselor, I can say it has not. Here are a few things that have remained constants in the twenty plus years that I have been in my position:

The Confidentiality Dodge

This is mental health's first line of defense. There is a reason for confidentiality. Clients need to know what they say to their therapists won't be repeated to others. Assured of confidentiality they are free to say anything, and subsequently, get to the point where they can resolve their problems.

Unfortunately confidentiality can be used to cover-up incompetence in the system. Whenever there is a horrific incident involving firearms, the media always focuses on the gun issue. I always wonder why the individual is walking the streets in the first place. People don't become mentally unbalanced overnight. Inevitably it is discovered that these individuals have been in the mental health system. Usually little more is known as confidentiality is cited.

Stigma

Stigma means people are reluctant to seek treatment as others will perceive them as being "crazy" or "wackos."

Undoubtedly this is true in many cases. But when a caseworker has 700 individuals on her caseload and individuals have to wait months to see a psychiatrist, it hardly seems like stigma and the reluctance to seek treatment can be blamed for the failures of the American mental health system.

Contract for Safety

This concept is so ludicrous as to be beyond belief. At school we will send suicidal students to mental health facilities for help. They return, sometimes in less than 24 hours, because they have "Contracted for Safety". What this means is that they have signed a paper saying that if released they will not kill themselves. Unbelievably the word of fifteen-year-olds, who were so distraught that they were considering killing themselves, is now accepted as a rationale for their termination of treatment. In reality it is to protect the mental health facility in case liability issues arise. Contract for safety leads to revolving door therapy.

Revolving Door Therapy

The length of stay in inpatient treatment for adolescents is frequently not determined by the severity of their problems. I have seen students with what I perceived to be very serious problems return to school so quickly that our school did not even know that they had been admitted. In these cases I will frequently receive a call from the teacher at the inpatient program requesting schoolwork. The teacher will add that this is a formality as the student has already been discharged.

In other cases I have seen students stay for extended time with what I perceived to be a less serious problem. In such cases I think, "They must have good insurance."

Drug and Alcohol First

I have said that 99% of Ian Ingram's recommendations for the Student Assistance Program were for a Drug and Alcohol evaluation prior to a mental health evaluation. This was supposedly to rule out a drug and alcohol problem and not for MH to shirk their responsibilities. The Student Assistance Program still exists although Ingram is no longer with it. But in 99% of the cases, no matter what the concern, students are still referred for a drug and alcohol evaluation prior to a mental health. I have contended for many years that students with D&A problems ALWAYS have a MH problem. In a society that continuously emphasizes the perils of substance abuse, anyone who still engages in such activities must have a mental health issue.

Mental Health Treatment Programs for Adolescents

I have had many students over the years return from day treatment programs. This is a program where students attend during the day and receive their education as well as therapy. Education is often haphazard. This is understandable with students being from different schools, different grades, some with learning disabilities, some lacking motivation, and the inevitable breakdown in communication and delivery of school work between school and program. What is not understandable is that therapy is haphazard as well. The omnipresent group counseling is available (maximum number of billable clients, minimum number of therapists). Individual counseling usually consists of a quick flyby from the psychiatrist. What I have heard too often is the lack of therapeutic activities: we shot pool and played video games. On one occasion I made a call to a program for a discharge meeting on one of my students. I called several times but the phone was always busy. I was unable to participate in the discharge meeting. Later I was told the phone was busy because the students were using it!

What Could be Done

What could have been done for Chris? What can be done for others with mental health problems? If Chris had been admitted into the assisted living program in 2001, maybe things would have been different. To keep someone from walking out of such a program, as he did at the Crossroads group home in 2000, or being thrown out as what occurred in Shippensburg in 2002, one would be mandated to the placement. Maybe an ankle bracelet could be used. Of course there would have to be legal grounds to do so. Some states have medication courts. If individuals do not take their meds, they are placed. Perhaps something similar could be set up to maintain placements.

Still, I don't know if this would be enough. Chris might very well have chosen to end up in prison. He is brain damaged. One must go back to the analogy I used earlier: if the pipes are damaged what good does it do to treat the liquid that flows within them? At every step of Chris's trek through the mental health system and then the judicial system, this biological problem went unacknowledged or ignored. My understanding is that a great deal of progress is being made on how the human brain works. What is needed is a stronger tie between the mental health system, the judicial system, and scientific researchers. Individuals with brain damage should be encouraged to work with those investigating the workings of the brain. Perhaps those incarcerated could be given time off their sentence for their cooperation with researchers.

Epilogue

Once when he was young, I was pouring out my troubles about Chris to my mother on the phone. Not knowing what else to say, she said it would be over some day.

After ten years, I finally earned my PhD in 2005. My research almost came to a complete halt during the bad days of 2001. My professors never knew the depth of my problems with Chris.

When I finished my dissertation, my committee asked me what I was going to do next. They hoped to hear that I planned to do research and pursue publication. I was fifty-three at the time and my adult life had been hard: working, the pursuit of the doctorate, and raising Chris. I told them it was time for me to have some fun.

Dancing had always been fun for me. After finishing my dissertation, I started swing dancing later in the year. I had done swing dancing at other points in my life. However, I always stopped when my partners left my life. This time I was determined to do it with or without a regular partner.

One of the great things about dancing is that I met a whole new set of people who knew nothing about my life as Chris's father. For the most part, they still do not. I continued with swing but branched out into other forms of dance as well: ballroom, tap, and even a little country line dancing. What a hoot! A man in his sixties learning how to tap dance! Dancing took my life in a new direction.

The partner thing took care of itself as well. As they say, when you are not looking for someone, you'll find somebody. We dance two or three times every weekend in the Harrisburg area with occasional road trips to Philadelphia, Baltimore, Washington, or Pittsburgh. We chaperone the prom every year. The last three years we have gotten the floor to ourselves for one dance to do a samba. When we finished the students gave us an ovation.

My father was not a dancer. He died in 2011. It made me think. At the funeral were his three children and his three biological grandchildren. The six are a good legacy for him to leave to the world.

I was distraught over his death. But my father, a former Marine Corps sergeant, was always big on doing what needed to be done no matter what. So I did what I knew he would have expected from me. I set aside my emotional distress and gave a eulogy that will be forever remembered by those that were there.

Afterwards, I thought of my own life. I would have no children of which I could be proud to be my legacy. I would have no child that would be capable of delivering a great eulogy.

When I was raising Chris, I did not want another child. He was enough. Now I hear peers talk with pride about the accomplishments of their adult children. I know they had their own trials and tribulations when their children were young, and now they can look back and feel that it was worth it. I cannot do the same. I had the trials and tribulations without the payoff. I wish I would have had another child.

A dozen years ago all of the students at Susquenita knew Chris. As the years have gone by, there have been gradually less and less that know of him. Some of the younger faculty members have never heard of Chris. Most of today's students are surprised to know that I ever had a child. Occasionally I encounter students who have parents who are incarcerated. I tell them about Chris. I emphasize the point it is not their fault their parent is in prison, and they can't make the parent change. The parent has to be willing to change.

I am coming to grips with the *legacy* thing as well. The students of Susquenita are my legacy to the world. I am now 63 and look forward to making a difference in their lives every day. Many of our students will be the first person in their family to go to college. I help them get there.

I have no immediate plans for retirement. I have started a program called "Susquenita Remembers". Every winter we collect photos from alumni from one decade in which the school was in operation for a permanent display. So far we have done the 50's, the 80's and the 90's with the other decades to come.

When I meet people my age, a general topic of conversation is children and grandchildren. I try to steer away from these areas. If unable to do so, I try to cut it off by saying my son lives in New Hampshire.

When I run into people that knew Chris when he was younger, they seldom ask about him. I am unsure if they know what happened to him, or if knowing Chris's past, they are afraid the answer will prove to be embarrassing for both of us. When they do ask I usually say one of two things. The first is the truth devoid of details: he hurt someone really bad and is in prison. The other is that he moved to New Hampshire to chase after a woman he met on the internet. This usually evokes a few chuckles and stops the conversation. Which answer I use depends on how I feel at the moment.

Occasionally someone asks if I ever regret adopting Chris. What I regret is not being able to help him. I regret not being able to break the perpetual dysfunction of the American mental health system.

Journal

October 2014

In my role as school counselor, I go to a discharge meeting on a fifteen-year-old student. He was attending school at a partial program similar to the one Chris had attended. He was receiving both education and counseling at the partial program. The student was not doing well in the program. His participation in both the educational component and the counseling component was minimal. Sometimes he would sleep. At other times, he was disruptive. He was reluctant to take responsibility for his actions. There was a family therapist at the meeting. He says the boy was not invested in therapy. Some appointments were not kept. His diagnosis: mood disorder, major depressive disorder, dysthymia disorder, substance abuse, and the possibility of borderline personality disorder. Recommendation? Send him home! I ask why he is not being placed in a more restrictive environment such as a RTF (group home). It was as if I said the emperor had no clothes. The room got very quiet. The person in charge, who was not the psychiatrist, mumbled something about giving him a chance. Some minutes later, when the meeting adjourned, as we walked out the door he whispered to me that he "half-way agreed."

End of Journal

Christopher's Story:
An Indictment Of The American Mental Health System

The perpetual dysfunction on the American mental health system continues.

Appendix

Psychotropic Drugs Prescribed to Chris

Medication for Chris Rubisch in chronological order. This list contains most but not all the medications that he has taken. Although some worked better than others, none were successful in treating his problems.

Imipramine 10 MG 11/89 2 times a day
Imipramine 25 MG 1/90 2 times a day
Dexedrine 5 MG 3/90 2 times a day
Methylphenidate 5 MG 4/90 2 times a day
Methylphenidate 10 MG 5/90 2 times a day
Thioridazine 9/90 35 MG 2 times a day
Methylphenidate 20 MG 10/90 2 times a day
Thioridazine 5/91 25 MG 2 times a day
Methylphenidate 4/91 5 MG third dose added
Prozac 20 MG 3/93 per day
Ritalin 25MG 11/93 weight 28.2 kg
Clonidine .1 mg 11/93
Ritalin 30 MG 7/94 1.02 MG/kg
Cylert 5/97 37.5 MG 3 times a day
Tegretol 5/97
Imipramine 25MG 7/97 1 tab bed for week, then 2 bed
Depakote 250 MG 9/97 1 tab 3 times a day
Dexedrine 5 MG 9/97 1 tab 4 PM
Dexedrine Spansule 10 MG 9/97 1 tab AM

Christopher's Story:
An Indictment Of The American Mental Health System

Lithium Carbonate 300 MG 10/97 1 tab twice a day
Lithium Carbonate 300 MG 11/97 1 tab a day
Paxil 20 MG 11/97 1/2 tab in AM
Adderall 20MG 11/97 1 tab twice a day
Risperdal 1 MG 12/97 1 tab twice daily
Lithium Carbonate 300 MG 3/98 1 tab 2 times a day
Lithium Carbonate 300 MG 3/98 1 tab 3 times a day
Methylphenidate 10 MG 12/98 1 tab 9 AM
Methylphenidate 20 MG 12/98 1 tab twice daily
Lithium Carbonate 300 MG 12/98 2 tabs twice daily 9 AM
& 9 PM
Risperdal 1 MG 12/98 1 tab twice daily

CPSIA information can be obtained
at www.ICGtesting.com
Printed in the USA
BVHW071322130121
597727BV00005B/636

9 781622 879762